PRAIS

WES "SCO(

AN_

THE BIG BANG, THE BUDDHA,
AND THE BABY BOOM

"A Mark Twain for our times, Nisker's book delivers exquisite guidance on liberating the mind while loving the world." —Joanna Macy, author of *World As Lover, World As Self*

"Wes Nisker joins the grand tradition of social historians casting a knowing eye at the absurdities of history . . . witty, insightful, soulful." —Daniel Goleman, former *New York Times* science writer and author of *Emotional Intelligence*

"Nisker is the consummate student/teacher, soaking up the world . . . and trying to make it a better place. Long may he chant." —Ben Fong-Torres, rock journalist for *Rolling Stone* and the *San Francisco Chronicle*

"A joyful, thoughtful romp of remarkable breadth . . . a wise, funny, and truly wonderful journey." —Jack Kornfield, author of *No Time Like the Present* and other spiritual classics

"Nisker's journey is a joy to read." —Paul Krassner, author of *Murder at the Conspiracy Convention and Other American Absurdities*

THE BIG BANG, THE BUDDHA, AND THE BABY BOOM

THE
SPIRITUAL EXPERIMENTS
OF MY GENERATION

WES "SCOOP" NISKER
FOREWORD BY ANNE LAMOTT

Monkfish Book Publishing Company
Rhinebeck, New York

Paperback ISBN 978-1-948626-90-3
eBook ISBN 978-1-948626-91-0

Library of Congress Cataloging in Publication Data

Names: Nisker, Wes, author. | Lamott, Anne, writer of foreword.
Title: The big bang, the Buddha, and the baby boom : the spiritual
    experiments of my generation / Wes "Scoop" Nisker ; foreword byAnne
    Lamott.
Description: Rhinebeck, New York : Monkfish Book Publishing Company, 2023.
Identifiers: LCCN 2022046211 | ISBN 9781948626903 (paperback) | ISBN
    9781948626910 (ebook)
Subjects: LCSH: Nisker, Wes. | Spiritual biography--United States. |
    Buddhists--United States--Biography. | Radio journalists--United
    States--Biography. | Baby boom generation--United States.
Classification: LCC BL73.N57 A3 2023 | DDC 204.092--dc23/eng20230207
LC record available at https://lccn.loc.gov/2022046211

Book and cover design by Colin Rolfe

Monkfish Book Publishing Company
22 East Market Street, Suite 304
Rhinebeck, New York 12572
(845) 876-4861
monkfishpublishing.com

CONTENTS

FOREWORD

I HAVE KNOWN and loved Wes Nisker since I was a girl in the San Francisco Bay Area in the sixties, although we have never met. He was the newscaster and political commentator on KSAN, reporting with amazement, rich insight, and hilarity on anything that might be of interest to the counterculture audience—or that instantly *became* of interest once he got his hands on it.

I loved the often joyous reporting, but even more, the spirit that wove together exhortation and travelogue, the matrix where evolutionary science meets the cosmic and the cause.

I have always loved his wild heart, his hippie joy, his riffs on society and the human condition, his own evolution from nice Jewish boy from Nebraska to cherished Buddhist teacher.

I loved his revolutionary social philosophy based on fairness and equality and love, and how respectfully he could help me understand Einstein and Buddha and complicated social theory, all aswirl with quotes from the Marx Brothers and Carl Sagan and Allen Ginsberg. He wrote, "If Gautama Buddha were around today, I am certain he would sprinkle his teachings with research findings from the evolutionary sciences. In the Pali Canon, the earliest record of the Buddha's teachings, he doesn't talk about gods or cosmic consciousness but instead tells us to investigate our body and emotions, the process of walking, hearing, seeing, and thinking."

I had never made this connection before, yet now it seems so obvious.

He is a philosopher, poet, mystic, gentle madman, comedian, and sage, and a great storyteller, and such an important influence on me and many others as we were beginning to find our writing chops. Using humor and getting away with it when writing about difficult topics is hard work. What he is doing and has always done is risky and hard, and he inspired countless people to try. He has such a great touch. Listen to this:

> In 1976 I flew to Japan to report on a music show called the Dolphin Project. The idea was to put on a big rock-and-roll concert and simultaneously educate Japanese kids about the plight of whales and dolphins. Performers included Jackson Browne, Ritchie Havens, Warren Zevon, Odetta, John Sebastian, Wavy Gravy, and others. The never-say-die hippies believed that rock and roll could help save whales, just as our

generation's protests and music may have helped shorten the Vietnam War.

Young Japanese jammed the Tokyo concert hall to hear the music, but they seemed indifferent to the whale exhibits set up on the perimeter of the auditorium. Interviewing people waiting in line for the show, I asked one Japanese kid why he had come. He replied, "To see Mister John Sebastian sing his song from *Welcome Back, Kotter*."

"And how do you feel about the whales?" I asked.

"Oh, the whales," he said, smiling enthusiastically. "They are very delicious."

His work, his comedy, his perspective and performance art have always been crazy wisdom, based on helping us learn both who we are, and how to serve the world's needy, including ourselves. He taught us meditation after a journey to India, he taught us how to laugh at our dear silly selves, and to get very serious and efficient in the face of our criminal politicians, climate disaster, environmental justice.

His book *Crazy Wisdom* is one I would take to a desert island to remember what is true about humanity and evolution and culture and myself. And *The Big Bang, the Buddha, and the Baby Boom* is a delicious consommé of similar brilliance, joy, pain, Buddhism, and life-giving humor. It really *is* about Buddha, and the Big Bang and the Baby Boom, among many other things, a story told in his unique and excitable voice, professorial when the situation calls for it or Borscht-belt and richly spiritual, with goofy tangents and theatre of the absurd and profound scientific proofs and exhortations and Hebraic laments, and soothing assurances that we all make sense somehow, and are all worthy of love.

That's the main thing Nisker teaches me: love. Love for you and my own disappointing self, love for the poor and this planet, love of curiosity and truth. He is the most entertaining newscaster in history, side by side with excitable social historian, spiritual guide, family man. And he can move me nearly to tears:

> We also know that we co-arise with the sun and the atmosphere and could not live apart from them. The energy that wiggles our fingers and moves our legs comes from the sun. Our bodies are even built out of Earth elements: Our bones are made of calcium phosphate, the literal clay of earth molded into our shape; the liquids in our body have the chemical consistency of the oceans; we literally sweat and cry seawater. This body is not mine. It is Earth's body. It is evolution's body. It's a loaner.

It is Earth's body. This guy breaks my heart with beauty.

Just to read his introduction will give you a working understanding of our evolutionary truth as humans. Go on; I dare you.

I think you will immediately understand why he has been loved for so long by his listeners, readers, students, and friends.

He is irresistible, one in a million, or as he would probably put it, just one in 8 billion, but man, has his light shone brightly, illuming our way.

Read this book and you will see why I have loved this man for fifty years now, loved the hope, the dharma teachings, the rock and roll, the agitation and comfort, and the great wit. I have often said that laughter is carbonated holiness, and the effervescent Wes Nisker is one of my favorite Holy men ever.

—ANNE LAMOTT

THE TIME OF YOUR LIFE

MINE IS NOT the "greatest" generation. Those who lived through the Great Depression of the 1930s and World War II laid claim to that title, leaving my generation of Baby Boomers with an impossible act to follow. Our struggles were more personal than those of the Greatest Generation and our enemies more elusive. We faced the great depression of physical and spiritual homelessness, and armies of psychological demons. We were born into an age in which the old stories were too old to have meaning anymore and the new ones still too new. We grew up in a society in which God was being doubted, truth was being disproved, and salvation kept changing its brand. We lived through so many revolutions—social, political, sexual, and scientific—that our heads are still spinning. Perhaps those of us born in the second part of the twentieth century could collectively be called the Confused Generations, and there are good reasons for that.

As we Boomers were growing up, radical ideas of modern science were entering public awareness. We heard about the theory of relativity, and even though most of us still don't understand what it means, it entered our 1960s culture as the mantra "It's all relative." And because it's all relative, then what is "real" and "true" and "good" became anybody's guess. The theory of relativity pointed us toward the ethics of "Do your own thing" and to the ultimate summation of relativity: *"Whatever."*

We in the post-World War II generation were taught by the new science to understand that physical reality is not what it appears to be. When we came into the world, Einstein and his cohorts had already made matter disappear. Poof! "Matter is energy," they said. The rug was pulled out from under us, and underneath the rug there was no solid ground to stand on. One of the great ironies is that at a time when our culture was thoroughly devoted to materialism, our scientists discovered that matter may not even exist.

We Boomers came into a world in which astronomers were discovering billions of galaxies filled with untold billions of suns, casting great doubt on our importance in the universe, shrinking us to nearly nothing. When we were born, chaos was still something that could be avoided if you were careful, but in our lifetime it turned out to be a law of nature. Furthermore, we arrived in a world that the physicists claim is governed by the law of indeterminacy, so how could we possibly have known what we were doing?

While the physicists were busy deconstructing reality, the anthropologists and historians were taking us around the world and into the past, showing us the vast array of beliefs and behaviors across human cultures. We could pick up *National Geographic* and learn about Siberian reindeer herders or social dance rituals from around the world, watch a TV show about the decline and fall of the Roman Empire, or read about the belief, once widely held, that the earth is flat (though that one is somehow still holding on).

In the process, another kind of relativity was revealed to us: We saw that our own moral codes and ways of life were socially constructed and not absolute truth. We realized as well that our knowledge of the world was tentative and that someday our culture's understandings might be considered primitive or laughed at by humans of the future, if there are any.

Which brings us to the fact that we've lived all our lives with some threat of doom hanging over our heads. We grew up with the prospect of thermonuclear war, to which was later added the threat of environmental collapse. We have lived under the shadow of the mushroom cloud and the fires of global warming. A potential apocalypse has been our constant companion for seventy-five years, and we've bequeathed our non-solution to Gen X, Gen Y/Millennials, Gen Z, and now Gen Alpha.

Boomers and more recent generations grew up in a culture that is, wisely, questioning its own mythology. In 1966, *Time* ran a cover story asking, "Is God Dead?" While the editors chose not to answer the question, the very fact that they raised it did not bode well for the deity. It seemed that even if God isn't dead, he was at minimum having a midlife crisis.

Many in my generation felt that our parents' belief system was kind of ridiculous, like believing in Santa Claus. Could there really be a supreme "being" who created everything and witnessed and judged our every action? We were deeply disturbed when God sanctified the slaughter of millions who didn't believe in a particular "Him," and many of us began to feel that the religious ceremonies we had to attend were, well, empty of meaning. So, we were left without divine support or even spiritual guidance as we began to confront the ominous and only relatively real world.

Added to our doubts about God and the universe were growing uncertainties about ourselves. We arrived on the scene when the immediate descendants of Sigmund Freud were busy taking apart the human psyche and showing us—in case we hadn't noticed—that our lives are not lived rationally, that we are controlled by unconscious drives and primal instincts. The psychologists told us that our parents were the cause of our miseries, a theory that—regardless of its accuracy—would form a wedge in what became "the generation gap."

In his book about Boomers called *Growing Up Absurd,* psychologist Paul Goodman wrote, "It was destined that the children of affluence, who were brought up without toilet training, and freely masturbating, would turn out to be daring, disobedient, and simple-minded." Maybe that's why we started chanting: "We want the world and we want it now!" We were poorly toilet trained and prone to tantrums.

To add insult to insult, in our lifetimes evolutionary biologists decoded the seed molecules of life and discovered that we are related not only to the great apes but also to the lowly bacteria. The Victorian era was shocked to hear Darwin's claim that humans were descended from monkeys, but we were the first generations to be told our mama was a germ!

And finally, those born in the last half of the twentieth century arrived at a time when technology, in all its forms—transistors, lasers, and integrated circuitry; autos and airplanes; radios, movies, TVs, personal computers, and smartphones—began to drive us, fly us, and seduce us far from our homes toward a global village that has no center and few traditions. We were born into a time of physical and metaphysical disruption, of aimlessness and uncertainty, and all the king's horses and all the president's men could never put it back together again.

Some who grew up in this time have since been wandering through the wreckage, trying to find a spiritual refuge or a mythology that fits the curve of our souls. The search has led many of us far from our Judeo-Christian roots and superpower citizenship to a faith in astrology or anarchist politics, in past lives or neopagan rituals, or to a devotion to nothing but the next thing. Some of what we found to believe in may seem superstitious or silly, but we desperately needed something to hold on to aside from our material possessions (which didn't really exist). We yearned for an authentic connection with each other, with nature and the cosmos, and many of us became devoted to that quest. We found ourselves involved in what Joseph Campbell called "the challenge of our time [which is] to forge a new story by which we might understand ourselves." Zen scholar Alan Watts defined the project somewhat differently: "We do not need a new religion or a new bible. We need a new experience—a new feeling of what it is to be 'I.'"

For me, as for others of my generation, the teachings of the Buddha spoke directly to my personal confusion. Many of us lived with a perpetual identity crisis, and Buddhist meditation promised to get to the bottom of the issue of "self" or, even better, beyond it. Buddhism also offered the solace of vast perspectives and methods to cope with the torrents of change we were experiencing. As Nietzsche said, "Buddhism is a religion for the end and fatigue of civilizations."

Out of our confusion and searching, we Boomers started a spiritual revival in the West known as the "New Age," which drew heavily on the Asian wisdom traditions. Closely aligned was the environmental movement, with its quasi-spiritual, neopagan overtones. Within these two loosely connected alternative cultures were a multitude of resources that may even contain the seeds of the new mythology or a new consciousness, came a different understanding of "I." We were the odd folks out when we went to Bodhgaya and Kathmandu in the '70s or the newly formed Zen Centers in California and New York, and we could never have imagined the next fifty years: the burgeoning mindfulness movement, the mass challenges to civil society, or people willfully ignoring climate realities we knew about half a century ago

This book tells a piece of the story of the genesis of these movements and the generation that spawned them. It is a personal account, illustrated by scenes from my life, and therefore circumscribed by my own interests and affiliations. It was my good fortune to work as a journalist in San Francisco for more than forty years, so I've had a great view of the action.

I was lucky to have been born in a time and place that provided so much freedom and material comfort, but life didn't turn out to be all that easy. Of course, the Buddha would say it's never easy unless we learn to see ourselves clearly. I hope this book will contribute to our clear-seeing so we can better understand ourselves and the world we share. *The Big Bang, the Buddha, and the Baby Boom* is dedicated to what I hope will be a legacy of the Boomer generation, now aging: renewed planetary health, lasting peace, love, connection, and enduring good vibes.

And, most important, I hope this book will serve as a reminder if not a rallying cry that we Boomers will keep fighting for the principles we lived in our youth—to our last breaths, for the sake of Gen X'ers, Y'ers, Zoomers, Alphas, and the many generations to come.

STARTING OUT CONFUSED

SOMETIMES I STAND in front of my little altar at home and have to shake my head in astonishment. How could a nice Jewish boy from Nebraska grow up to have an altar filled with "graven" images? There's no golden calf on my altar, but there is a statue of the seated, meditating Buddha from India; a wooden head of the Chinese laughing Buddha; a picture of the Hindu goddess Kali; a wooden statue of the Native trickster Coyote; a Thai potency amulet; and various nature fetishes. Also, on my computer is a statue of Ganesha, the Hindu elephant deity who brings good fortune.

Other images and pictures get shuffled onto my altar and desk from time to time, and I admit that sometimes I get confused. For instance, Hinduism, one of the sources of my mythological melting pot, has designated different gods and goddesses to deal with different human dilemmas. So what if I call on a deity who doesn't work on the particular problem I'm having that day? This confusion would not arise with Jehovah, an all-purpose God.

Speaking of Jehovah, as I was looking at my altar one day, I realized that I may simply be in recovery from monotheism. I grew up with a very strict God-the-Father creating a somewhat dysfunctional mythological family, and that may be why I became spiritually promiscuous.

Looking at my altar, I recognize also that most of these deities are illegal immigrants: None of them has a Green Card to work in America. Many have been smuggled into this country, and mostly by people like me, citizens of empire who traveled around the colonies looking for new ways of being and praying.

I should make it clear that I don't quite believe in the figures on my altar as entities that exist in some nonearthly realm. They simply represent qualities of being or attitudes of mind that I admire or wish to develop in myself. Furthermore, my primary spiritual path for the past fifty years has been the philosophy and meditation practices of Buddhism, which, in the form I have adopted, has very little to do with deities.

Still, why did this same Jewish boy begin studying Buddhist meditation, a practice that involves sitting on the floor rather than on a nice, soft couch? The Jewish people let their forelocks grow as a sign of piety; the Buddhists shave their heads. Jews wail and beat their breasts in front of their God; Buddhists sit silently in cool detachment. Of course, it's impossible to know for sure why anyone gets called to mystical pursuits. Some sages say that such a calling is the result of past lives and accumulated good karma. Scientists may eventually discover that it has something to do with genes and that people attracted to mysticism have a weirdly twisted double helix shaped like a yin-yang symbol. All I know for certain is that some mixture of circumstances pulled me around to the other side of the planet, back through the centuries, and into the lap of the Buddha.

Like many members of my generation, I've been somewhat obsessed with studying myself and have spent a good deal of time and money trying to discover the roots of a lifelong sense of alienation. Just being alive in this time of rapid change is enough to make anyone feel disconnected, but each of us has our personal stories to help explain the condition.

I was born and raised as the only Jewish kid in a small Nebraska town, so I was an outsider from the very beginning. Perhaps learning that role in childhood is what eventually led me into league with the radicals and jesters of the world and then into journalism, where I could stand outside and witness the action, and finally into Buddhism, where detachment is considered a state of grace.

Could all this have happened because I was the only kid in my hometown who didn't believe in Jesus? For a while, when I was a young boy, there were just enough Jews in Norfolk, Nebraska, to keep a little synagogue going above the local bakery. As I remember, you walked around behind the bread ovens and up a flight of wooden stairs to a large room with wood-slat walls. At one end of the room stood the Torah and facing it, a few benches. I recall the bakery smells wafting up to this makeshift synagogue on Friday nights and making it very difficult to fast on Yom Kippur. In the early 1950s, two of Norfolk's Jewish families moved away, which left too few Jewish males in town to form a *minyan*, the minimum number of ten who must be praying before God will listen. The synagogue over the bakery had to close down.

. . .

In order to prepare me for my bar mitzvah, my parents hired a traveling rabbi, the Jewish equivalent of the circuit preacher. His name was Rabbi *Falik,* which may partly explain why he did not have his own pulpit and congregation but was relegated to traveling by Greyhound Bus through the small towns of Iowa and Nebraska, ministering to the lost Jewish tribes of the American Midwest.

Once a week, the bus would stop right in front of my house, and out would come Rabbi Falik, who looked as though he belonged in a European *shtetl*, wearing long forelocks and a big black hat and overcoat, even in the summertime. I didn't want my friends to see this medieval-looking man coming to our house, so whenever he was due I would lure them away from the neighborhood and then make up some excuse to run back home just in time to meet the bus and rush Rabbi Falik inside.

My bar mitzvah lessons exemplified my early spiritual confusion: I was memorizing long passages of transliterated Hebrew script that made no sense to me in preparation for joining a Jewish community that in my hometown did not even exist.

In order to take part in the youth life in Norfolk, I had to become a mock Christian. I joined the Presbyterian Youth Fellowship and even sang hymns and carols with them at the annual Christmas vespers program. However, when the songs mentioned Jesus as "our lord" or "savior," I would secretly cross my fingers. I wanted Jehovah to know that I had not fallen for this hoax and that I was still waiting for the real messiah to come. My parents didn't want me to feel left out of the fun at Christmastime, so every year they brought a tree into our house, which we decorated with lights and bulbs. But we called it a Hanukkah bush and always put the Jewish star of David on top of the tree. I remember taking pride in the fact that we Jews had one more point on our star than the Christians did, perhaps proof that we were the chosen people. I was looking for any reason to believe.

My parents had arrived in Norfolk during the Great Depression. One of my mother's relatives, a rag merchant, had wandered all the way from Russia to this little Nebraska town, where he opened a clothing store. He invited my father to move to Norfolk and start up a shoe department in the store, and since times were tough, my father accepted. Even though he knew nothing at all about shoes, suddenly he found himself fitting them onto the feet of German and Polish farm wives.

My parents planned to wait out the Depression in Norfolk and then move back to Minneapolis, where, as my mother would wistfully say, "There is more *Yiddishkeit*." But one thing led to another, and before you knew it my father had his very own store, Nisker's Shoes and Accessories, right there on Main Street, and had joined the Norfolk Country Club, the Lions Club, and even the Masonic Lodge. It is odd and yet somehow appropriate that a bloodline of Jews who were driven out of their Middle Eastern homeland two millennia ago would eventually arrive in the American Midwest, only to get involved with the Masons, a European mystery cult based on Middle Eastern myths.

In some ways, my father's childhood was not that different from my own. He grew up in a village outside of Warsaw, Poland, where he was one of the few Jewish kids in a rural Christian community. His parents had owned a small grocery store, and they lived very simply, just a half step up from the peasantry. Of course, as recently as 1906, the year my father was born, the majority of the world's people were simple peasants. For most of history, only royalty and members of the aristocracies have lived in the style to which so many of us today have grown accustomed.

My father had personal experience of this economic truth. When I was growing up, one of his favorite sayings was, "We live like kings here." Our family would be sitting around the kitchen table (made of Formica), eating a dinner of meatloaf with a side dish of canned peas or Jell-O, and suddenly, with a satisfied and somewhat awed expression on his face, my father would look around at us and say, "We live like kings here."

Of course, satisfaction in life is always geared to expectations, and like many of my generation, I grew up with great expectations, believing that with the right breaks I could own everything I wanted and even live happily ever after. My curse was perhaps one of too much choice. There were so many things to desire, so many sensual pleasures to experience, so many identities and lifestyles from which to choose. As Franz Kafka wrote, "You are free. That is why you are lost." Maybe it is precisely because I had so much to desire that I eventually began to desire nothing less than the end of desire itself, which is the goal of the Buddhist path. But my kingdom still eludes me; my Shambhala remains hidden, somewhere behind the billboards in this land of plenty.

My spiritual search began in earnest sometime in early adolescence, and at age twelve I had what might have been my first revelation. I was spending a lot of time in the News and Tobacco Store on Norfolk's Main Street, reading the latest comic books and peeking into the girlie magazines whenever the proprietor wasn't looking. One day I was startled by a face staring out at me from the cover of a magazine, and for a few moments I stood transfixed. Only later in life, after years of studying Daoism and Buddhism, did I realize that I had seen the face of my first guru, Alfred E. Neuman.

Alfred E. was the young absurdist prince of the Western world, the great American teenage tantric master, forever grinning at me and my generation from the cover of *Mad* magazine. His look is one of both detachment and bemusement as he watches over our mad, *Mad* world without concern, knowing that all is sham and fakery and that this too shall pass. No matter what kind of cartoon apocalypse is going on around him—the whiz-bang-crash kerplunk-varoom of falling empires, brutal wars, political summit meetings, important movie spectacles, significant fashion trends, and ever-increasing entropy—Alfred E. never stops grinning. And all he ever says is "What, me worry?" the most succinct statement of cosmic realization ever spoken. The *mad* mantra.

Unfortunately, as an adolescent I must not have understood that Alfred's "What, me worry?" is a rhetorical question. So I often found myself answering back, "Yes, me worry." Maybe I just should have practiced Alfred's grin and the mental state would have followed eventually.

> *"Einstein pronounced the doom of continuous or 'rational' space, and the way was made clear for Picasso and the Marx Brothers and* Mad *magazine."*
>
> —MARSHALL McLUHAN,
> *The Medium Is the Message*

I grew up very confused about who I was and how I fit into the scheme of things. The esoteric religious traditions claim that the spiritual path begins with the question "Who am I?" and my childhood seems like a perfect primer for that inquiry.

During my high school years, my parents sent me to a Zionist summer camp in the piney woods of Wisconsin, hoping that I would meet other Jewish kids my age and discover my Jewish identity. It worked. The first few times we gathered at Camp Herzl's flag circle, I felt a secret thrill at the realization that everyone around me was Jewish. Not one of these kids believed that Jesus was the messiah!

At Camp Herzl I became more comfortable with being Jewish, but that identity threw into question my qualifications as an American. The camp counselors told us that as Jews our true home was in Israel, the land of milk and honey promised to our people in the Bible. Every day at camp we raised the Israeli flag and sang the Israeli national anthem, and our cabins were named after *kibbutzim* in Israel. Camp Herzl made me think that maybe I belonged in the Middle East, not the Middle West.

The communal camp experience itself was a thrill for Norfolk's lone Jewish boy, what with everybody singing and eating together and each group of cabin mates bonding like a tribe within a tribe. Meanwhile, we learned about the kibbutzim, the communal farms in Israel where people shared everything and lived as one big family. On a kibbutz there were theoretically no rich or poor members and no competition for money or power; everyone worked and played together, united in a common goal. That sounded like a great idea to me at the time, and despite all the socialist experiments that have since failed, it still sounds to me like a good idea. So call me a socialist and blame it on Camp Herzl.

Socialism is indeed a part of Jewish heritage, being the brainchild of European Jewish intellectuals and labor leaders, and I believe the socialist vision is a legacy the

Jewish people should be proud to own. We might some-day yet regard Karl Marx as highly as we do Groucho.

A Tibetan holy man once told me that I was probably the reincarnation of an Eastern European Jew who had been killed in a Nazi concentration camp. According to this Tibetan,

I suffered so much under the Nazis that a lot of my negative karma was burned away. That's why I was rewarded with rebirth here in America, the land of the free and the home of the plenty. In this life I have been given great physical comforts, copious education, and enough money and leisure time to discover the teachings of the Buddha, setting me on the path to complete liber-ation from the rounds of rebirth. In other words, if I use this new incarnation well and become fully enlightened, I won't have to be born again in Europe, America, or even Tibet. I will be freed from the suffering of incar-nation, which Beat Buddhist Jack Kerouac called "the wheel of the quivering meat conception."

I am highly skeptical when it comes to any stories about rebirth. Reincarnation might just be another of the fictions humans have invented to make sense of this puzzling existence and the apparent lack of justice in the world. Then again, if there is rebirth, maybe I should keep my nose relatively clean during this lifetime to ensure that my next one is quite spectacular. I could consider being good as a form of "next-life insurance."

$$\left(\; 2 \;\right)$$

GENERATION

gen-er-a-tion: *1. The act or process of bringing into being; 2. (a) all the people born and living at about the same time; (b) a group of such people with some experience, belief, attitude, etc., in common; 3. The stages of successive improvement in the development of a product, system, etc.*

—WEBSTER'S NEW WORLD DICTIONARY

EACH GENERATION HAS a collective personality, shaped by its moment in history. Both of my parents endured the lean and fearful times of the Great Depression and then the tensions of World War II, and they understandably became obsessed with security—physical, political, and social. Their children, however, were born into relative affluence, with our freedom and physical well-being somewhat assured and our range of opportunities expanding rapidly.

America was the world's new superpower superstar, and my birthright, along with that of many other white middle-class boomers, seemed to include the possibility of pursuing any career and achieving any amount of wealth, success, or fame. But life has never been easy, and our biological programming simply may not have been able to accept the degree of security and plenty that was offered to us. Maybe that's why so many of us grew restless and began asking, "But what does it all mean?" We had to come up with some impossible struggles of our own.

The official optimism of 1950s America was focused on prosperity, growth, and expansion: Everything was going to get bigger and better, more spectacular and more fun. The advertisements of the time, whether for Bendix carpet sweepers, Bayer aspirin, or Buick automobiles, were selling not only the product but also the fantasy of the perfect family in their own home, among many possessions, living happily ever after.

In his book *The Fifties,* Robert Heilbroner writes that the postwar decade saw the transformation of capitalism into consumerism; owning became a religion, a reason for living. Jesus may have said, "Give up all you have and follow me," but American free enterprise was saying, "The more you have, the more blessed you are."

We might have understood, at least subconsciously, that the life we were facing was not as promising as it seemed in the advertisements. Many of us saw our parents working too hard at jobs they didn't like, cautious about every penny they spent, hanging on to deadened marriages, stuck in perpetual planning and paranoia. We didn't necessarily want to model our lives after them, and, because of the opportunities held out to us, it seemed that we wouldn't have to.

Meanwhile, at the core of my adolescent experience, and that of many friends whom I have spoken to, was a deep loneliness. Many of us were growing up in our own separate bedrooms, in single-family houses, separated from extended family or community ties. The ancestors of humans moved in packs, and so did we for a very long time, and perhaps it was too strange to suddenly be raised in such isolated conditions, within so many private spaces and moments. I know that I, for one, was lonely, and my parents didn't understand me, and God seemed either remote or unlikely, so I went searching for something I could not yet name. So did a lot of other young Americans, and what we found, at last, was each other.

Sometime in the mid-fifties, a youth culture began to emerge in America, centered on the image of rebels and lost souls and driven by the beat of rock-and-roll music. Kids were given the keys to the family car and drove around town blasting rock songs on the radio, all the while looking for each other and the sex and excitement that this wild new music promised. "Oo-wee, oo-wee baby, oo-oo-wee..."

Those early rock-and-roll lyrics may have been silly, but the music itself was immediate and visceral, pulling you into the moment and into your body. The new sound was electric and had a resonance that penetrated the brain and activated the spine: If you turned it up loud enough you could feel yourself alive in a whole new way, a feeling some would later try to stimulate through various body therapies and kundalini yoga experiences.

The songs were about love and sex and celebration, and few of us could refuse the invitation to join the dance. The tribal beat of rock and roll was the first rumbling of a pagan revival that would eventually lead to love-ins and nature worship and the New Age. "Oo-wee, oo-wee baby, oo-oo-wee..." While the music was making us dance, television and the movies were supplying us with multiple virtual realities: many possible lives to be lived, roles to be played, dreams to be realized. The postwar generations were largely weaned on television, going right from the breast to the boob tube. So we were able to leave home before we left home: to join Robert Young's family or the Nelsons; to be a Mouseketeer or visit Buster Brown or Mr. Rogers's neighborhood; to live for a while in the world of cowboys, gangsters, or space travelers. These were all fairly glamorous and exciting places compared to home, filled with characters that outshone our parents or teachers. There is little doubt that those media experiences contributed to the identity issues and self-questioning of recent generations. As Marshall McLuhan said, "We shape our media and then our media shape us."

For many of us, the characters who appeared in our mediated realities became our heroes and heroines, and often they were renegades. On movie screens in the 1950s, the perky, socialite banter of Cary Grant and Fred Astaire was replaced by the mumbling of sullen, scruffy characters played by Marlon Brando and James Dean, who captured the growing restlessness and disaffection of young Americans. These sensitive new heroes were determined to find their own truth and even create a new identity for themselves. After all, becoming whoever you want to be was also part of the American dream, and if you could choose, why would you want to put on a gray flannel suit and work for some corporation until you die? You might as well get on a motorcycle or into a fast car and have some thrills and excitement.

Anyone who was an avid reader, as I was, might have also been tantalized by the nonconformists who appeared in the books of J. D. Salinger, Herman Hesse, and James T. Farrell, some of which were assigned reading in school. Equally alluring to me were the highly publicized real-life exploits of authors such as F. Scott Fitzgerald, Ernest Hemingway, and Henry Miller, whose worlds seemed full of a kind of passion and intensity that could only be found on the edges of society.

The allure for many of us was somewhere, anywhere, outside of the mainstream. Writer Norman Mailer described the new rebel: "the hipster, the man who knows that if our collective condition is to live with instant death by atomic war ... or with a slow death by conformity with every creative and rebellious instinct stifled ... why then the only life-giving answer is to accept the terms of death, to live with death as immediate danger, to divorce oneself from society, to exist without roots, to set out on that uncharted journey with the rebellious imperatives of the self."

The mythology that I absorbed through the media was that life should be high drama, fraught with significance. The lives of my heroes, whether on the screen or the pages of books, were condensed into moments of emotional intensity, and their stories were all about the quest for love, money, or power. The message was that either there was intensity in your life or you weren't really living.

For some the call to rebellion also included the sound of laughter and scorn. My own disaffection was fed by a group of comedians and satirists: Steve Allen, Sid Caesar, Ernie Kovacs, and a little later, Lenny Bruce and Mort Sahl. Since I had never felt entirely at home in American society, I loved hearing it ridiculed, and since I sensed that life itself was absurd, I identified with those who could laugh at it all.

For some, awakening from the American dream led to a deep cynicism. An old saying goes, "Scratch a cynic and you'll find an idealist," and that may be especially true of mid-century, middle-class youth. After we saw several utopian visions turn out to be mirages, a cynical attitude arose to provide protection against any more false promises: it was a dark, safe place to hide.

For others, the idealism became deeply ingrained, and the possibility of living happily ever after continued to haunt us through the years. After first giving up on material wealth as salvation or the possibility of ever perfecting American society, some of us decided to save the planet and maybe even turn it into a paradise or else find nirvana and move in there. For many of us, it seems, there was always another utopia just around the corner.

3

A BRIEF HISTORY OF OUR SELF

> *"Americans cling to the myth of individualism as though it were the only normal way to live, unaware that it was unknown in the Middle Ages and would have been considered psychotic in classical Greece."*
>
> —ROLLO MAY, *The Cry for Myth*

I WANTED TO escape myself. That's one reason I went looking for some kind of cosmic consciousness. I yearned to feel part of a bigger reality so that I could leave the small reality I was living in—the separate, subjective, "me" monad. It was painful just being little old me. And I was not alone in my aloneness: A lot of other monads also desperately wanted to feel connected to something.

Many postwar middle-class children were pumped up with self, pampered and prompted to become special someones, to have it all, to be anyone they wanted to be. The most common advice given to me by my parents was to "be somebody" and "make something of yourself," as if I was nothing just being who I was. Meanwhile, the media promoted the idea of being unique, someone who stands out, and the rule of the economic game was that "you make it on your own." My peers in the sixties youth culture told me to "do your own thing"; the messages of the seventies were "find yourself" and "express yourself." Individuality was emphasized even within the countercultures, where a new communal ethos was also being promoted. I believe that, for many of us, the focus on the individual self was so extreme that we tried desperately to escape that single identity. "I need some *self*-help! Get me to group therapy, meditation, tribal events, rock-and-roll concerts—anything!"

Recent generations in the West have been shaped by the pressures of individualism. Perhaps never before in history have people felt so much on their own, without what anthropologists call "participation mystique," a sense of being part of a tribe or community, nature, the cosmos, or the divine. In his book *Constructing America, Constructing the Self,* psychohistorian Philip Cushman writes, "The masterful, bounded self of today, with few allegiances and many subjective 'inner' feelings, is a relatively new player on the historical stage."

Crucial to a sense of self is the feeling of individual freedom, which barely existed in most premodern cultures. An individual was born into a certain religion, occupation, social status, and geographic area—and that was that. There was no such thing as upward mobility and hardly any sideways or outward mobility. No one could conceive of switching to a religion that better suited their personal convictions, and very few thought they could choose an occupation, spouse, or a hometown. If you approached a medieval peasant or even a member of a tribe wandering around in the desert just a hundred years ago and asked, "What do you want to do with your life?" that person wouldn't have known what you were talking about. Not until the second half of the twentieth century did the notion that you could be anyone you want to be in this lifetime become so widespread.

At one time, people did not even believe that they were in charge of their own mind. In his now-famous study, *The Origin of Consciousness in the Breakdown of the Bicameral Mind,* Julian Jaynes claims that in early Greek culture "the gods take the place of consciousness." Jaynes cites passages from the *Iliad* that indicate that the Greeks who lived circa 1000 *b.c.e.* "have no will of their own and certainly no notion of free will." According to Jaynes, the early Greeks heard their thought process as voices of the gods, an interpretation that today we would call schizophrenic. Even Agamemnon, the king of men, did not believe in his own power, saying, "Not I was the cause of this act, but Zeus. Gods always have their way."

Five hundred years later, we witness a radically new "self" emerging in the Hellenic world, as Socrates, Plato, and Aristotle heralded the apparent power of each individual to manipulate the contents of his or her own mind. It was no longer the gods' voices that we heard inside our heads but our own. A similar shift of identity took place when the early Christians began to emphasize each person's soul and its private salvation or damnation. It was no longer the tribe's history that was important, as in the Old Testament with the Jews; the focus shifted to the individual.

The thoroughly modern Western self truly came alive during the sixteenth and seventeenth centuries in Europe, in the era known as the Enlightenment, poorly named according to most Buddhists. The Enlightenment thinkers became so enamored of their powers of intellection and invention that they declared themselves virtually independent from the external world. They took power away from God and truth away from the church and gave everything over to human reason and science. With Enlightenment consciousness, individuals grew more identified with their own minds, which were seen as the source and center of the personal self.

Although this modern Western "self" went through its adolescence in Europe, it reached full maturity in America. In fact, the first time that the word *individualism* appears in print was in Alexis de Tocqueville's book *Democracy in America,* published in 1835. How much larger does the individual loom today in America, the land of individualized license plates?

According to Robert Bellah and his associates in their classic sociological study *Habits of the Heart,* the contemporary American identity can be traced to two streams of individualism: utilitarian and expressive. Another name for utilitarian individualism is the "Protestant ethic," which emphasizes the qualities of endurance, stoicism, and self-reliance. ("Self-Reliance" is the title of Ralph Waldo Emerson's most famous essay, which spoke clearly to the Americans of the nineteenth century.) Expressive individualism, a legacy of the romantic movement, placed great value on the unique and passionate "soul," which feels deeply and lets its feelings be known. The early American poet Walt Whitman was the champion of expressive individualism, beginning his famous book *Leaves of Grass* with the line "I celebrate myself." That sentiment still echoed through the "me" decades of the late twentieth century and on into the New Age ideas of self-realization.

The postwar generations have been dealing with symptoms of an extreme form of self-focus, which is perhaps why ours has been called the "culture of narcissism." As Philip Cushman writes, "Psychotherapy theories from the 1960s through the 1980s described a self similar in most ways to the self displayed in television commercials, magazine ads, and the blockbuster sixties musical *Hair*... a self that was exhibitionistic, self-involved, thoroughly acquisitive; it valued emotional expressiveness, a lifting of political and personal constraints, and immediate gratification."

The modern self that lives in us at the beginning of the twenty-first century has an extreme sense of its own autonomy and separateness. In the mirror of our culture, and in the mirror of our private bathrooms, we see only the individual, which is, of course, a completely distorted image of reality. We think and act as though we are independent of the external world, outside of any context or gestalt, whether that of a god or evolution. Upon examination, we find that this sense of selfhood is a kind of delusionary state, a bizarre form of schizophrenia in which we label all of the different voices in our heads as "I" or "mine." Believing them all to be ours is as far-fetched as believing they all belong to God.

Ironically, while many of us seem completely lost in our individual dramas, our culture has become acutely aware of how interwoven we are in the fabric of all things, from the atoms we share with the stars and the stones to the DNA molecule we share with all other living beings to the growing awareness of how much our behavior is inherited from the life that came before us. We know we are inseparable from the great streams of biological and cosmic evolution, a part of the whole, and yet we wander around in what Alan Watts called our "skin-encapsulated egos," sensing ourselves from moment to moment as isolated and autonomous. Our intellectual understanding of who we are is therefore completely out of sync with our felt sense of ourselves. I believe that this dissonance is what led many of us to seek help in the Asian wisdom traditions, which emphasize seeing through the individual self into the interrelatedness of all things.

The modern self that we carry inside us is a phenomenon of nature and history. We can't blame it on Descartes, Adam Smith, Whitman, Dr. Spock, or anybody else. Besides, with all of its faults, this modern self has brought with it the development of extraordinary social and political freedoms as well as great material comforts. Few of us would trade places with a medieval peasant, even if it meant having a deep feeling of interconnection with the world, since the world we would be deeply interconnected with would be that of a medieval peasant.

Nonetheless, it is increasingly clear that our modern self is somehow out of balance. Our perceived separation from the world has grown much too extreme, and as a result both we and the world are suffering. One major problem with our "masterful, bounded self" is the outrageous belief that we are completely in charge of our lives and that we can have it all or become whomever we want to become. These notions are accompanied by almost inevitable frustration and cynicism when things don't work out the way we imagine they should. God used to be a kind of sacred scapegoat for our failures, but for many of us there is no longer anyone to blame but ourselves. That is why this modern self is not very easy to live with.

Out of the feelings of separateness and isolation came our political and spiritual searching: at the heart of our various movements were the twin acts of expressing ourselves and fleeing from ourselves.

Perhaps recent generations' experiments with drugs, communal living, and new psychospiritual practices are attempts to escape from our solitary confinement, to relieve the burden of being someone special. That would explain the fact that during the seventies, Baby Boomers were flocking to est seminars, where they were told that they were all nobodies. The boomers seemed to welcome this message: what a relief to be nothing, a nobody. Meanwhile, the right drug could evoke a feeling of connection to the world, and sometimes even an experience of oneness. The group rituals of rock-and-roll concerts or political gatherings offered a sense of belonging; group therapy sessions could create an instant, intimate community; Asian spiritual practices promised to dissolve the illusion of separateness.

One of the reasons I began Buddhist meditation practice was to find relief from the constant burden of self-focus. It's ironic but somehow natural that I would reject individualism mostly for selfish reasons. I fled from the emphasis on self, not so much for lofty social or spiritual ideals, but because it didn't feel good.

The Buddha's teachings have spoken to many in the West today perhaps because he shows us that our suffering is directly related to our self-involvement. Buddhist meditation practices are a way to loosen our intense identification with our own drama, and they offer both relief and a corrective to our civilization's extremes of selfhood. The growing popularity of meditation may be a sign that the evolving self is now seeking a new equilibrium, a middle way. It just might be that self-consciousness has become masterful enough to see through its own hubris, and we are coming to a saner and more satisfying understanding of who we are in the world.

4

THE COLLEGE OF YOUR CHOICE

THE METAPHYSICAL ADVENTURES and spiritual searching of recent generations can be blamed, in part, on our "good liberal arts education." In college we were given vast overviews of history and civilizations, taught how to be skeptical, and given the tools to deconstruct any truth we might have been holding.

My parents wanted me to go to college so that I could "get ahead" and maybe someday join that highly respected class of people known as professionals. I wouldn't just be a merchant buying and selling things; I would have something to profess, a calling. What they didn't realize is that a good liberal arts education can lead you to doubt everything your family and society ever taught you.

In a college class on the "worldly philosophers," for instance, I was assigned to read Karl Marx, who explained that capitalism is based on greed and competition and offered a supposedly more humane way to organize society. In an introductory psychology class, I read the essential works of Sigmund Freud, who informed me that human behavior is mostly governed by unconscious fears and desires, causing me to doubt my own reasons and motives. In a literature seminar, I read Samuel Beckett, who wrote, "Nothing is more real than nothing," implying that reality itself was a questionable concept.

When I started college I really didn't know what I wanted to do, so I majored in the humanities, with a special emphasis on philosophy. I was hoping to discover some explanation for this life I was living.

I slogged through the Western philosophers, all of them giants of thinking: Plato, Aristotle, St. Augustine, Spinoza, Kant, Descartes, Berkeley, and Locke. I tried to digest their brow-bending, mind-twisting attempts to figure everything out, until finally in my senior year I was allowed to take a seminar on the existentialists, and they informed me that all previous Western philosophy was bunk and nonsense! Too late. If only I could have taken that seminar as a freshman, I would have saved myself a lot of thinking and my parents a lot of money.

In my late-college angst and turmoil, I read the existentialists with great excitement—books with titles like *The Plague, Nausea, No Exit, Fear and Trembling, The Sickness unto Death, The Concept of Dread.* I felt as though I had found my mentors: the philosophically depressed. And even though the existentialists were full of despair, I found them a lot more fun to read than Kant or Descartes.

The existentialists said that God was dead or, as Nietzsche put it after looking with dismay at the world,

"God's only excuse is that he doesn't exist." Reading statements such as these supported my own doubts about a personal God and sent a shiver of exhilaration through me, as if I were part of something new and subversive. After all, denying God seemed somewhat dangerous back then.

The existentialists also concluded that life and the universe were absurd and that humans could not discover truth or meaning through the rational mind. What a relief it was for me to read that! It wasn't my fault that I couldn't find any good answers; human beings simply aren't smart enough to figure out why we are here. What I found most fascinating, however, was that the existentialists saw the rational mind as part of our problem. The curse of the human condition was precisely this desire to figure everything out. As Albert Camus wrote,

> If I were a tree among trees, a cat among animals, this life would have a meaning, or rather this problem would not arise, for I should belong to this world. I should *be* this world to which I am now opposed by my whole consciousness and my whole insistence upon familiarity. This ridiculous reason is what sets me in opposition to all creation. I cannot cross it out with a stroke of the pen.[1]

The existentialists led the coup (off with our heads!) against Western metaphysics. It's as if they turned Descartes upside down and said, "I think, therefore I am not," having concluded that the act of thinking—reason itself—was getting in the way of just being. And above all else, the existentialists wanted to be. To be! That secular anti-intellectual ideal would inform all subsequent Western art and philosophy and become the cornerstone of the mid-twentieth-century countercultures. It would help open the door to Eastern mysticism and its practices of "nondoing" and "just being" and would eventually lead to the hippie "be-in," which was nothing less than a joyous attempt to ritualize the existential ethos. As Jean-Paul Sartre wrote, summarizing the dilemma and all previous Western philosophy, "Being has not been given its due."

Unfortunately, the existentialists had no way to break out of their rational minds. There were no meditation classes for Nietzsche or Sartre, no Dalai Lama around to say, "Hey, Camus, take it easy. Just try paying attention to your breath for a while." For the most part, the existentialists remained depressed, martyrs to the game of reason.

Of the existentialist philosophers, Camus was my favorite. I carried *The Myth of Sisyphus and Other Essays* around in my pocket for months, reading it over and over as if it were scripture. At the end of his own search for meaning, Camus had found absurdity, and he held it out like a banner, a secular challenge to the existential warrior: Can you live without God or meaning? I had no idea whether or not I could, but it seemed I would have to try.

Lucky for me, I was setting out on my search for meaning at a time when the Asian wisdom traditions were beginning to gain serious attention in the West, popularized by the novels of Herman Hesse and the books of scholars like Alan Watts. I discovered that for centuries the Daoists, Hindus, and Buddhists had also emphasized being and nonthinking. Furthermore, I read that the Asian sages had developed elaborate ways to actually practice being, methods that would teach you how to break free of your mental machinations and bring you right into the moment, the now.

I wondered what it would be like to just be. Who knew? I began to fantasize about traveling to Asia and studying these unfamiliar practices. It even occurred to me that I might be able to get a master's degree in being. A Zen masters.

> "I teach about one thing, and one thing only: the
> causes of suffering, and the end of suffering."
> —GAUTAMA BUDDHA

In the 1960s the teachings of the Buddha started becoming popular with young Westerners. Perhaps it was because we felt some deep resonance with the story of Prince Siddhartha, the Buddha-to-be, who left a life of great ease and abundance in his father's palace to seek a completely different kind of happiness. Many of us who had grown up in this land of plenty and who still found life somewhat empty or meaningless could certainly relate to Siddhartha's decision. We may live like kings here, as my father said, but is that what life is all about?

Buddhism may have appealed also to the young American's desire to rebel against society. Just the practice of meditation—sitting still and doing nothing—was a kind of defiance, a rejection of our culture and its purposefulness. Furthermore, Buddhism did not demand a belief in any god or ideology, and many of us didn't want any more of that.

Of course, if you had been experimenting with your mental states through the use of drugs, then Buddhism offered an exotic new way to conduct those experiments. It held out the hope that you could get high and never have to come down, the fulfillment of the bohemian's wildest dreams.

As I read books on Buddhism in my late-college years, I also remember being attracted to its commonsense, no-nonsense approach to human dilemmas. Like my own scientific culture, the Buddha asked us to strip away all beliefs and to take a good, hard look at the facts of life. What was required was a deconstruction of all realities, including the process of thought and, ultimately, the thinker as well. To begin following the Buddha's path, everything had to be laid bare.

The Buddha begins his teaching by telling us that ordinary life is a condition of suffering. That is his First Noble Truth. It doesn't matter if you are rich or poor, strong or weak, smart or dumb: Being alive—just getting a body and nervous system—means that you will feel pain, hunger, fear, sexual desire, sickness, old age, and death. On top of that, being human means that you will take all of the above-listed conditions very personally. The Buddha holds our gaze on these truths, repeating them over and over again in his teaching so that we won't live in illusion and become so attached to the drama of our existence.

Perhaps the First Noble Truth was a good antidote for our idealism, especially useful for Americans who had come to expect too much happiness from a life of relative comfort and abundance. The First Noble Truth can also remind you that you're not the only one who isn't mastering this life. You are not the only one who isn't getting it all together or living happily ever after. Misery loves company, and most of us take some consolation in the fact that dissatisfaction is not ours alone but is built into the very conditions of existence.

Like many others with whom I've spoken, I find great comfort in contemplating the Buddha's First Noble Truth, and over the years I've continued to reflect on its meaning, especially during times of personal troubles. Eventually, I fashioned my own litany of our difficult living conditions, which offers the traditional Buddhist insights into suffering with a modern, scientific slant.

The litany begins with the fact that we have very little choice over our existence. Consider that we didn't ask to be born, or at least we don't remember asking. Furthermore, each of us was born with a powerful survival instinct, which makes us want, more than anything else, to stay alive. So we didn't choose to be born, and we feel strongly compelled not to die. It's as though nature has trapped us in this life.

We also don't get to choose the body that we will inhabit during our lifetime. I don't remember any catalog of choices being offered, such as, "Would you like eyes in the back of your head?" or "Do you want to swim, fly, or walk as your primary means of locomotion?" Meanwhile, according to the geneticists, our DNA carries information that determines how tall we will grow, how strong our teeth will be, what diseases we might contract, and how long we are likely to survive. Like it or not, you get issued a particular body which has its own life to live, regardless of your desires.

At birth you are also given the face that you must wear until death (unless you can afford a new one). So you got a droopy chin or a strange-looking nose or a nearsighted squint. My curse is somewhat low-slung ears, and in high school one of my witty friends got a big laugh when he said, "If your ears were any lower, Wes, you'd have to use deodorant on them." But whatever facial features you get will surely influence how the world looks at you, which in turn affects how you look at the world.

We also don't get to choose much about our personality. The evolutionary psychologists have found that each of us is born with a certain temperament: a tendency to be cautious or novelty-seeking; motivated either to avoid harm or to get rewards. And the psychologists tell us that whatever part of our personality isn't determined at birth will be set solidly in place long before we are old enough to have much choice in the matter. And we don't get to select our biological parents and/or the dear ones who raise us and shape these lifelong neuroses.

What it comes down to is that we are not *free* to be ourselves; we *are forced* to be ourselves. And no matter what our personality or living conditions are like, life is not all that easy. We have to fight gravity every morning when we get out of bed and with every step we take; we have to feed these bodies a few times a day, which means we have to work hard finding food or making money to buy it. The survival instinct keeps us moving, working, schlepping.

To top it all off, we are never told why we are here or exactly what it is we are supposed to be doing while we are here. And we are given just enough consciousness to know that we do exist and that someday we will die, which we very much don't want to happen. These are the basic conditions of our lives.

Who created such a universe? As the Hasidic rabbis used to say, "If God lived on earth, people would break out all his windows." Or, as Wavy Gravy says, "If you don't have a sense of humor, it's just not funny."

Although I was attracted to the Buddha's honesty about the suffering of life, what really seduced me was the possibility of release from that suffering. After laying out the facts of life, the Buddha describes how we can train our minds to be relatively free of desire and fear: We can loosen our attachment to our genetically and culturally programmed self-importance.

While the First Noble Truth had spoken to my darker, cynical side, the Buddha's offer of liberation spoke to the idealist in me. Here was the old promise of happiness, and not in heaven above or in some ideal society that seemed nearly impossible to construct anytime soon. Instead, the Buddha was pointing to the happiness that comes from within ourselves and is present here and now. It all made good sense to me, and I began to wonder where the trailhead was to get started on the Buddha's path.

5

THE DOWN BEAT

"Maybe the Beat Generation, which is the off-spring of the Lost Generation, is just another step toward that last, pale generation, which will not know the answer either. In any case, indications are that its effect has taken root in American culture."

—JACK KEROUAC

MANY YOUNG WESTERNERS, including me, were led onto the Buddhist path because we were following the fresh footprints of the beatniks, the bohemian heroes of our own culture. In the early 1960s, anyone listening for the sound of a different drummer might have heard a beatnik's bongo drum, already growing faint and beginning to be drowned out by folk rock music (electric guitars were just tuning up in the Haight-Ashbury); but there was at least one bongo still being beaten in a pad in San Francisco's North Beach or New York's Greenwich Village by some mustachioed guy in dark sunglasses, a cat so cool you could hardly see him. At least that was the essential image of the beatnik, and it seemed inviting to many restless young souls, even if we didn't quite understand what was going on behind the glasses.

The all-American beatnik was television's Maynard G. Crebs, a dopey-looking guy trying to emulate a European intellectual and failing miserably. *Dig?* That stereotype continues to obscure the real impact and importance of the beatnik movement, although it was barely a movement at all. At its core and responsible for its ongoing influence were just a few writers, mostly poets, who laid the foundations for the cultural upheavals of the second half of the century and announced the beginning of a neoromantic, spiritual revival in America.

It is true that the Beat writers were undisciplined and self-indulgent, but they were much more than rebels without a cause. The Beats were, as Allen Ginsberg once said, "beatifically beat down." In other words, they were spiritual outcasts, driven into cellars and coffeehouses by the cold emptiness of materialism and the forward rush of progress. What they began to express, in an American idiom, was a message of universal love and compassion. They were naive mystics, in love with life and the mystery and seeking their own ecstatic visions.

Although their political challenges would reverberate through several decades of American history, perhaps the Beats' most important contribution grew out of their adventures in Hinduism and Buddhism. They made the teachings of the Asian wisdom schools sound contemporary and accessible to young Westerners like me.

Through their writings they introduced exotic words like *karma, dharma, nirvana,* and *mantra* into the hipster's lexicon.

Each of the Beat writers seemed to find an Asian spiritual path that perfectly suited his or her temperament. Allen Ginsberg was attracted to the colorful, flamboyant Hindu tradition and personally took on the role of the wandering sadhu who travels around chanting the names of god. Gary Snyder, the serious poet-scholar, was drawn to Zen Buddhism, where discipline was required and mind could be used to penetrate mind. Meanwhile, Jack Kerouac seemed to find solace for his own agonies in Indian and Tibetan Mahayana Buddhism, which emphasized compassion for the suffering of all beings.

It was Kerouac who captured and opened my heart during my college years. I've reread him again and again and am still moved by his aching attempt to love the world in spite of all the suffering he saw. I felt Kerouac's dilemma as similar to my own, just as I had felt Camus's to be, but Kerouac was a generation closer to me, working in the fresh milieu of American cultural experimentation.

As a writer, Kerouac was the American Joyce, with complete access to his melodious flow of mind, singing out jazz-inspired colloquial prose that spoke to a generation just beginning to experience other rhythms, both on and off the page. More important, Kerouac awakened me and many others to the possibility of a new kind of freedom and the joy of being present in each moment for the thrill of life itself. He turned the highway into a spiritual path, and just reading him made me want to jump in a car and head for a farther shore, in search of what he called the "golden eternity." Many would follow in Kerouac's tracks, and as early as 1958 in his book *The Dharma Bums,* he prophesied what the hippie saga would look like:

> a world full of rucksack wanderers, Dharma Bums refusing to subscribe to the general demand that they consume production and therefore have to work for the privilege of consuming, all that crap they didn't really want anyway. I see a vision of a great rucksack revolution, thousands or even millions of young Americans wandering around with rucksacks, going up to mountains to pray, making children laugh and old men glad, making young girls happy and old girls happier, all of 'em Zen Lunatics who go about writing poems that happen to appear in their heads for no reason and also by being kind and also by strange unexpected acts keep giving visions of eternal freedom to everybody and to all living creatures.[2]

Of that group of Beat poets, Gary Snyder was the one who took meditation most seriously, and in the middle of the Beat hoopla he disappeared to Japan for almost a decade to study Zen. Upon his return to America, he started a Zen center in the Sierra foothills and in 1969 published *Earth House Hold,* subtitled *Technical Notes and Queries to Fellow Dharma Revolutionaries.*

In this book, which became popular in the burgeoning counterculture, Snyder described how personal, spiritual work is an essential part of political transformation. He also brought together Native American and Zen Buddhist views of the natural world and in doing so began to lay down a metaphysical context for the coming environmental movement. In an interview for the *Southern Review,* Snyder expressed his vision:

> As a poet I hold the most archaic values on earth. They go back to the late Paleolithic: the fertility of the soil, the magic of animals, the power-vision in solitude, the terrifying initiation and re-birth, the love and ecstasy of the dance, the common work of the tribe. I try to hold both history and wilderness in mind, that my poems may approach the true measure of things and stand against the unbalance and ignorance of our times.[3]

Throughout the last half of the twentieth century, many newspaper photos featured Allen Ginsberg sitting on an open-air stage, beard flowing and beads jangling, his harmonium droning while he intoned a mantra meant to exorcise America's injustices and greed. It may be that Ginsberg did more to bring Hindu and Buddhist culture to the West than any of his contemporaries simply by chanting *om* at countless political protests and demonstrations from the 1960s onward.

Along with an entire generation of young Americans, I was both shocked and excited by Ginsberg's notorious poem, "Howl." Here was someone from our own culture, speaking like an old Hebraic prophet, denouncing the gods of war and commerce that had taken over our nation's soul. Ginsberg named the evil "Moloch" and threw down the gauntlet:

> Moloch the crossbone soulless jailhouse and congress of sorrows! Moloch whose buildings are judgment! Moloch the vast stone of war! Moloch the stunned governments! Moloch whose mind is pure machinery! Moloch whose blood is running money! Moloch whose fingers are ten armies! Moloch whose breast is a cannibal dynamo! Moloch whose ear is a smoking tomb![4]

Ten years after Ginsberg wrote those words, the United States was conducting the Vietnam War and Ginsberg had become an elder spokesperson for the antiwar movement and the hippies. Once he suggested that everyone over the age of fourteen take acid, "including the President and our vast hordes of generals, executives, judges, and legislators of these States. They should go to nature, find a kindly teacher or Indian Peyote chief or guru guide, and assay their consciousness with LSD."

The Beat poets confronted a latter-day version of the same industrial civilization that had once been opposed by William Blake and the romantics as well as by Thoreau and Whitman and the transcendentalists, all of whom the Beats drew on for inspiration. They answered the same call to love and celebrate life, in contrast to trying to conquer and control it.

Although Gary Snyder could offer a brilliantly logical and statistic-filled critique of environmental policy and Allen Ginsberg had vast files of research into the misdeeds of the CIA and FBI, especially in areas of drug policy, the message of the Beat writers transcended politics. It was a universal call to love and compassion, to a new consciousness that included all people and all species. The Beats, and the hippies who followed them, were trying to stage a spiritual revival in America, to start something life affirming in the seemingly perpetual last days of Western civilization.

For many young Americans it was the Vietnam War, not the promise of nirvana, that first turned them toward Asia. From the mid-sixties to the early seventies, Vietnam was at the center of many lives, whether fighting for or against the government of the United States. Every night on the news we watched the relentless US bombing of a small nation on the other side of the world, with all of the bloody horrors of war and increasing American casualties and no clear justification for it all. If you were mildly disgruntled or disaffected, then seeing the escalation might have been the final straw that caused you to drop out and join the ranks of radicals and hippies or at least the antiwar movement. Several friends have told me that they began protesting after seeing photos of the Vietnamese Buddhist monks burning themselves to death in protest.

My major concern during the Vietnam War was avoiding the draft, and like others I stayed in school primarily for the deferment it offered. In the spring of 1967 I decided that I couldn't tolerate another college seminar. After rejecting the option of shooting myself in the foot, I decided to see a shrink at the University of Minnesota, where I was enrolled in graduate school, and to fake a psychosis. I was hoping to get a letter saying I was crazy and therefore unfit for military service. The university assigned me to a psychologist whose name was—*Dr. Dredge.*

I came to our first meeting with my head bowed, looking really sad, my hands shaking badly enough that I could pretend to be embarrassed by their twitches. Occasionally I would jerk my head up with a startled look, as if I had suddenly been reminded of something unpleasant.

Dr. Dredge watched this show with pity. I told him that my symptoms could be attributed to the fact that I had taken several bad acid trips and that my latest one included a vision in which the entire earth had become a bed of quicksand. Even worse, this vision kept returning without warning; sometimes while walking along, I would suddenly be afraid to take another step. Dr. Dredge had heard about LSD flashbacks and was sympathetic. After about five sessions he agreed to write a letter saying that I was too crazy to kill. Uncle Sam believed him, and soon the mail brought me the magic classification 4F.

Having successfully dodged the draft meant that I could stay at home and struggle against the Vietnam War in America, the "belly of the beast." A few months later I took a trip to California, where the hippies were supposedly really hip and the revolution had already happened.

6

FLOWER CHILDREN

"The youth of today are really looking for some answers—some proper answers the established church can't give them, their parents can't give them, material things can't give them."

—JOHN LENNON

PERHAPS BECAUSE OF the Vietnam War and the protests against it, many people remember the hippies as a political movement. Others focus on the sex and drugs, and some even blame the hippies for the moral decline and substance abuse problems that followed. At its core, however, hippiedom was a spiritual phenomenon, a big, unfocused, revival meeting.

Evidence can be found in the *San Francisco Oracle,* a Haight-Ashbury then-underground newspaper, which announced the first "Human Be-In" with the following manifesto: "The spiritual revolution will be manifest and proven. In unity we shall shower the country with waves of ecstasy and purification. Fear will be washed away; ignorance will be exposed to sunlight; profits and empire will lie drying on deserted beaches."

This was the true hippie agenda: a "spiritual revolution." A *be*-in.

Being a hippie was kind of like being in a new religion. We didn't exactly believe in a god—but we celebrated all the gods and goddesses. The ideas of Joseph Campbell and Carl Jung were in the air, and we understood that all the old religious stories were just stories, which meant that we could embrace them all as beautiful creations of human longing and imagination.

If you went to a hippie music concert or commune, you might see every spiritual tradition represented: images of Egyptian pyramids, Stars of David, Christian crosses, pictures of cherubs, Masonic icons, African tribal masks, Daoist yin-yang symbols, dreamcatchers, nature fetishes, and the list went on. Along with images of a Native American smoking a pipe, and several mul-tiarmed Hindu deities, one of the most visible symbols of the hippie religion was the Buddha in all his various poses.

The hippies were mythological collage artists, bor-rowing from various religions and cultures—whatever spoke to us or fit our fancy. Maybe we just wanted to feel connected to something: the universe, our bodies, the natural world, the movement of the planets, the mystery itself. Since we couldn't seem to make these connections in our churches and synagogues, we started looking for them on the fringes of society and in other spiritual traditions. We turned to ancient pagan and mystical practices of meditation, breathwork, sweat lodges, tarot and astrology, music and drugs.

The hippie was full of optimism and sweet innocence and wore clothing of many colors, leading to the designation "flower child." The beatnik costume had been working class, with old denim and black sweaters and the ever-present sunglasses through which to view the world darkly, and the punks and hip-hoppers would later return to dark fashions, but only after the colorful hippies had dragged bohemia out of the shadows for a brief moment in the sun. The hippie was a bohemian of a different stripe.

Hippie politics were simple; some would call them naive. We had no economic analysis or five-year plan: We simply wanted a transformation of consciousness and a world of peace, love, and good vibes. Was that too much to ask? Of course we didn't know what we were doing—any more than anyone ever does—but we did our best to articulate our vision. When I asked yippie leader Abbie Hoffman for his views on socialism, he replied: "I think that all 'isms' should be 'wasms.'"

If hippiedom was a religion, its primary ritual was the psychedelic rock concert. These were not all that different from the rituals of many sacred traditions: For centuries, people have ingested psychoactive plant substances and then danced in trance to loud music. The hippies were intuitively following this time-honored method of transcending ordinary reality.

Beginning at the Avalon and Fillmore ballrooms in San Francisco, the psychedelic rock concerts provided a setting for visionary journeying, or "tripping." Even the posters promoting the concerts were filled with images of transformation: humans sprouting flowers or antennae, buildings morphing into plasmatic beings, pictures of Native American warriors or Hindu deities. Often you had to be in an altered state just to read the posters announcing the names of the bands that were going to appear at the concert.

The visual component of the psychedelic rock-and-roll ritual was the light show, which made the walls pulsate with color and imagery. Often there were just patterns of swirling or gelatinous blobs of light that kept pulsing and changing, but if you were on the right drug and in a partial trance from the electronic music, these lights could represent subatomic realms or the organic world of cells and molecules. We had read about these invisible realities in newspapers and textbooks, but at the rock shows you could sometimes feel as though you were living inside them.

The music was the energetic engine, and usually the sound was loud enough to be felt as well as heard. In the rock show, you were in a vibrating universe, an aural space that drove everything out of your mind except the moment. All boundaries and distinctions could dissolve, and it was possible to have a vivid experience of oneness, as real as any that happened to any mystic who ever lived. As music critic Joel Selvin wrote in *Monterey Pop*:

> After one more chorus, he presses his guitar
> up against his stack of amplifiers, feedback

screaming, and dry-humps the back of the guitar. He slips out of the strap and drops to his knees, the guitar flat on the stage, and sprays lighter fluid over the face of the instrument. Bending down, he gives the guitar one quick kiss goodbye and ignites the fluid. Flames dance in front of him. His fingers flutter encouragement. He grabs the flaming Fender by the neck and breaks it apart on the stage, swinging it wildly. The pieces are discarded—burnt offerings—into the audience as he staggers off the stage and into history. Jimi Hendrix has played the Monterey Pop Festival.[5]

My first visit to California was in June of *1967,* to attend the Monterey Pop Festival, one the first of the large outdoor rock-and-roll celebrations. I was living in Minneapolis at the time, where a friend of mine had started publishing an alternative music magazine called *Twin Beat,* a sort of Midwestern *Rolling Stone.* He wanted to do a story on the Monterey festival and asked me to come along for the ride.

As soon as we pulled into Monterey, we became ecstatic. Our counterculture group in Minneapolis was very small, but here in Monterey were thousands of young people wearing their swirling psychedelic tie-dyes, the multicolored flag of hippiedom. Others were dressed up as cowboys or Indians or Edwardian ladies and gentlemen or whoever else they wanted to be at the moment. We saw people laughing in cars, dancing in the streets, everyone flipping peace signs to each other. The Beatles had just come out with *Sgt. Pepper's Lonely Hearts Club Band,* and everywhere you went, carloads of hippies had their windows rolled down and their radios blasting out the title song, everyone singing along as loud as they could. We were part of a new culture, a new world dawning: we were a force to be reckoned with. "We hope you will enjoy the show."

In Monterey that weekend, a giant, twenty-foot-high Buddha had been erected at the main entrance to the festival grounds. Every concertgoer was also greeted with the gift of an orchid as they entered. (One hundred thousand orchids had been flown in from Hawaii for the event.) The festival's theme was "Peace, Love, and Flowers."

The unnamed ingredient in the theme was, of course, drugs, and, for the three days of the festival, the marijuana smoke at the fairgrounds was thicker than the morning fog. If you looked deeply into a passerby's eyes, which you often did, you would as likely as not meet dilated pupils and that dazed-amazed look of someone who has just landed from another planet.

Even with all the drugs, there were hardly any arrests that weekend, probably because the police assigned to the event were continually being kissed by the hippie girls. By the end of the festival, most of the officers were wearing flowers in their hats or on their gun belts.

From the very first day, a rumor had been spreading that the Beatles were going to make a surprise appearance. Whenever a helicopter flew over the stadium people would shout, "It's the Beatles! They're here!" On the last night, the excitement mounted as the Mamas and Papas, the final scheduled act, took the stage. The evening had begun with Janis Joplin, tearing up the crowd with her version of "Ball and Chain," followed by a still relatively unknown British band called the Who, who closed with a song called "My Generation" and shocked the audience by smashing up their instruments right there on stage. Then came that legendary Jimi Hendrix performance in which he burned his guitar during his final number, a scorching, screeching version of "Wild Thing." The Mamas and Papas had to follow all that with their folk-pop ballads, but they did all right anyway and had the crowd singing and swaying along with "California Dreamin'." Still, everybody was waiting for the Beatles! We were Sgt. Pepper's Lonely Hearts Club Band, and they were our conductors.

Finally, after the second encore, Papa John Phillips stepped up to the microphone and said he had a very special announcement to make. The crowd gasped as he continued, "I have the great pleasure of presenting a very special treat here in Monterey tonight. Everybody please give a warm welcome for…" By now the crowd was screaming so loud we could barely hear Phillips finish his sentence, "Scott MacKenzie, here to sing his hit song, 'If You're Goin' to San Francisco, Be Sure to Wear Some Flowers in Your Hair!'"

Most of us sang along with MacKenzie's hippie anthem, but, as we used to say, "What a bring-down."

. . .

We didn't need marijuana to see through what Terry Southern called all the "ole bull-crap" in America back in the 1960s, but it may have eased the nausea that seeing through it induced. The middle-class, postwar generation was college educated and was starting to challenge our government's policies as well as the self-righteous view of Western history held by our parents and teachers. We had learned that America was built on the bones of Native peoples and that sixty million buffalo were slaughtered in less than one hundred years as our immigrant ancestors "settled" the continent. We studied about the crime of slavery and were aware of the ongoing racism in all areas of American life. And most damning of all, every day on the television news, we watched our government intensify the war in Vietnam, as America seemed to inherit and perpetuate the brutal, imperial ways of our European ancestors.

My parents were blind to America's faults. Perhaps they were too deeply scarred by the recent horrors in Europe to question the country that had given them refuge. In America, after all, they were finally enjoying security and freedom, especially in comparison to places like Moscow and Dachau, so they didn't want to rock the boat.

For a while in the 1960s and 1970s, I felt completely estranged from my biological family. I was a radical and an atheist. I had my astrological chart read, did gestalt therapy during which I once beat up a pillow that represented my mother, and of course, wore my hair long. Whenever I went back to Nebraska for a visit, as I did on the way back from Monterey, my mother would shake her head in disbelief and say, "When are you going to do something about that hair?" The other thing she'd say was, "When are you going to become staple?" She meant "stable," of course, but it always made me imagine myself as a paper cutout stapled down somewhere, and I shuddered to think of it.

Instead, inspired by the huge tribe of hippies I'd seen in California, I let my hair grow even longer. I wanted to join up full-time with this amorphous band of visionaries and thrill-seekers, and long hair was the unmistakable badge of membership. Soon after Monterey, I pulled up my Midwestern roots for good and moved to San Francisco. My blood relatives and my nation didn't understand me. I left home and joined a generation.

THE WHOLE WORLD
IS LISTENING

SAN FRANCISCO WAS the perfect place for a spiritual renaissance. Located far from the political power centers of Washington, DC, and New York, and even farther from the European religious and intellectual traditions, the Bay Area was a kind of remote outpost of Western civilization.

I really wanted to be a beatnik when I arrived in San Francisco, but I was too late to make the scene, so I was assigned to the hippies instead. To this day, I consider myself a kind of mongrel bohemian, with a beatnik head and a hippie heart.

It hardly mattered when you arrived: In the last half of the twentieth century, San Francisco was an ever-evolving anarchist convention and coming-out party. In the late sixties, youth rebellions were taking place all across America, in Mexico City, London, and Paris, but San Francisco was the spawning ground of the alternative metaphysics as well as the center of the celebration. It was Jerusalem and Babylon rolled into one. It was the place where disillusioned young people came together to create some illusions we could our own.

. . .

A few months after moving to the city, I got a job as a newscaster on a counterculture radio station, KSAN-FM. For a few years before the profiteers took over, KSAN and stations like it across the nation were rightfully termed "underground" radio. We criticized the government, made fun of old-time religions, encouraged the use of marijuana and LSD, and of course, played the music to accompany all of these activities. We were tribal radio, filling the heads of American youth with a call to rebellion and celebration.

The programming at KSAN reflected the growing counterculture interest in Asian spiritual traditions as well as various esoteric myths and rituals. Every day the morning disc jockey threw the I Ching and gave a full astrology report. As news and public affairs director, I would interview the Buddhist, Hindu, and Sufi teachers who were beginning to come through town more frequently in the late sixties, offering the Western hippies new ways to pray and get high.

The disc jockeys at KSAN took on funny, fictitious names: Reno Nevada, Dusty Street, Voco, Edward Bear, and Tony Pigg. Tony gave me my own radio name, Scoop, after I broke a story in San Francisco about the Chicago conspiracy trials. Our radio names were part of the counterculture theater, where everyone was free to fashion his or her own character. We were all playing with our identities, trying to "trip each other out."

Listening to tapes from those days, I am amazed that KSAN was allowed to continue broadcasting. The fact that the government did not shut us down is a testament either to the power of the First Amendment or to the inefficiency of the FCC and FBI. It could also be that we just weren't that important to anybody but ourselves.

I was KSAN's news director from 1968 through 1970 and continued doing features and documentaries for the station until 1979. In my early years as news director, I was usually the entire news department as well, which meant gathering news, writing it, splicing tape together, and doing the announcing.

I was not on some ideological mission, but like many people at the time, I was consumed by a fervent desire to stop the Vietnam War. However, as the counterculture's radio station, KSAN and its news department began to function as a communication center for not only the antiwar movement but also the Black Panthers, the Young Socialists, and even the Weather Underground. While my first news broadcasts were mostly satirical, I soon turned to serious calls for activism and protest and began to sign off my programs with the slogan, "If you don't like the news, go out and make some of your own." Being radical became part of my job description.

Marshall McLuhan called radio the "tribal drum," and that was certainly true for those who began to identify themselves as part of the hippie tribe. Although my newscasts became an essential element of KSAN's programming, the main message of the station was always the music. Hippies and radicals alike were caught up in the spell of the new rock and roll, the heartbeat of our common generational revolt. We told each other "they can't bust our music," meaning that no matter how much the authorities would squelch political protest, we would always be able to get messages of freedom, justice, and flower power out to "the people" through rock-and-roll songs. How wonderfully innocent we were. "T-t-t-talking 'bout my generation."

In the early days of KSAN, I used rock-and-roll music to punctuate and add emotional intensity to my newscasts—maybe inserting Bob Dylan singing "Masters of War" into a story from Vietnam or a line like the Jefferson Airplane's "Got a revolution, got to revolution"—from their song "Volunteers"— or the Youngbloods singing, "Everybody get together, try to love one another right now." The rock songs were our liturgy, our anthems, the *internationales* for the youth of the world.

To create a newscast, I'd sometimes take a tape recorder out into the streets and talk to people about a current issue, then mix their voices in with the politicians' speeches on the subject, add the statements of a few cartoon characters and some sound effects, and put it all together over a rock song or Indian raga. Often I would reedit a politician's words to reveal either the hidden truth or the essential nonsense of what was being said. Presidents Johnson and Nixon spoke in very regular cadences that made it fairly simple to edit or change the order and sense of their words. In the editing process I found that political rhetoric has rhythm, even if it doesn't have soul.

Sometimes, of course, the speeches needed no editing, and I could just play a certain phrase over and over for ironic effect. I once made a tape loop of Richard Nixon, with his usual bombast, saying, "No power on earth is stronger than the United States of America today, and none will ever be stronger than the United States of America in the future." Following that statement was the sound effect of thunder and lightning.

There were constant on-air drug references at KSAN, and listeners would occasionally hear the unmistakable sound of a DJ taking a drag off a joint. Marijuana smoking was perhaps our audience's most commonly shared behavior, a continuous Delphic ritual that helped make us into a tribe.

For a while, I was in charge of editing the on-air reports from Pharm Chem Labs, a commercial chemistry lab in Palo Alto that put out a weekly review of the drugs available in various neighborhoods around the Bay Area. The idea was to warn people of bad acid, badly cut cocaine or heroin, marijuana that was extra strong or had been sprayed with something toxic, and so on. The Pharm Chem people never moralized; sometimes, in fact, they sounded like today's radio wine connoisseurs, recommending good buys and excellent vintages.

A typical report went something like this: "In the Haight-Ashbury this week we have reports of a bunch of methamphetamine cut with baking soda. People should also be cautious about the Thai stick being sold in Berkeley in recent weeks. You may not be used to this much THC at one time."

Pharm Chem also provided a service whereby KSAN listeners could find out exactly what it was they had bought on the street before ingesting it. For a fee, you could send in a small sample of your drugs along with a five-digit number and then a few days later call up for a chemical analysis.

For a while KSAN was supported mostly by advertisements from record companies and rock promoters, along with a few hip entrepreneurs trying to reach the growing counterculture population. Often, to make extra money, the air staff would help produce the commercials for these sponsors. I produced a few ads for Undulator Waterbed Company, which, believe it or not, was one of eleven different waterbed companies advertising on KSAN during the first few months of 1977. Among their competitors were Magic Mountain Waterbeds, Waterbeds Unlimited, Neptune Waterbeds, White Tiger Waterbeds, Pasha Pillow Waterbeds, Embryo Waterbeds, Waterbed and Company, Waterbed Factory, Environmental Valve Waterbeds, and Porpoise Mouth Waterbeds. The hippie tribes were obviously conducting their cultural experiments in comfort. To paraphrase Emma Goldman, "If I can't sleep in a waterbed, I don't want to be in your revolution."

As KSAN began making real money for Metromedia, a battle began for the soul of the station. The on-air staff tried valiantly to maintain its counterculture principles and the integrity of the station's underground sound. When told to play a public service announcement for the military, for example, we all refused. I remember one disc jockey trying to reason with the station manager, saying, "Hey, man, you've got to realize that people are tripping out there in front of their radio. I don't want to be the one to bring them down with an army recruitment ad!"

. . .

Throughout the centuries, many peoples of the world have used various plant and mycelial substances in order to alter their consciousness. Most of this usage took place in conjunction with the spiritual life of the community, with the substances administered during elaborate rituals led by tribal shamans. Starting in the 1960s, outside of any formalized setting or guidance, a considerable number of young Westerners began to experiment with psychoactive substances: marijuana, mescaline, psilocybin mushrooms, and LSD. Although these were often consumed in a secular context, the substances still did their work and brought many people vivid experiences of the moment or of oneness or some other perspective on reality.

Research in molecular biology gives us clues to the connection between THC, the psychoactive ingredient in marijuana, and the actual experience of getting high. It turns out that the body produces its own version of THC and that the human brain and nervous system have a whole network of receptors for this cannabinoid-like substance. That means you've got a stash inside of you right now, and even in Red States, nobody can bust you for it.

Our body's natural THC was discovered by Israeli neuroscientists, who named it anandamide, from the Sanskrit word for "inner bliss." The scientists believe that our system produces this THC equivalent to aid in pain relief, for mild sedation, and also to help us forget. It is very important that we forget, because if we remembered everything that registers on our senses from moment to moment, we would be flooded with memory and could not function. So anandamide helps us edit the input of the world by blocking or weakening our synaptic pathways, our memory lanes.

Since the THC in marijuana is stronger than the natural version, and smoking marijuana brings in a huge dose all at once, the effect is to create a more complete short-term memory loss. The preconceptions we usually bring to experience are therefore no longer as available. That may be why stoned people often make those unusual connections in their brain, coming up with wild ideas that are so often experienced by the high person as profound but later may seem mundane or even silly. Also, when you are high on marijuana, you have temporarily forgotten what a sunset looks like or what ice cream tastes like, so you are experiencing these things as if for the first time.

The cannabinoids seem to have the ability to restore an innocence to our perception of the world, and people who have smoked marijuana often have a renewed sense of wonder and interest in whatever appears before them. In his book *The Botany of Desire,* Michael Pollan writes, "The cannabinoids are molecules with the power to make romantics or transcendentalists of us all." Marijuana may be a gateway drug—to mysticism.

The neurological explanation of getting high may help explain why a generation of potheads decided to start meditating and doing yoga. Marijuana offered a more vivid experience of the present moment by creating what is known in Zen as "beginner's mind," but as people in the drug culture used to say, "You always have to come down." When we began to read about the Hindu and Buddhist practices of being in the moment, we saw the possibility of the eternal now, of endless moments of forgetful, selfless bliss.

The real maker of mystics, however, was LSD. On October 6, 1966, right after LSD was declared illegal, a broadside denouncing the act was posted in the Haight-Ashbury district of San Francisco, bearing the following Prophecy of a Declaration of Independence:

> We hold these experiences to be self-evident, that all is equal, that the creation endows us with certain inalienable rights, that among these are: the freedom of the body, the pursuit of joy, and the expansion of consciousness, and that to secure these rights, we the citizens of this earth declare our love and compassion for all conflicting hate-carrying men and women of the world.

For many serious Western Buddhist and Hindu meditators, the psychedelic drug experience accounted for at least a few degrees of their turning eastward. Mushroom and peyote derivatives or LSD could give people at least the temporary ability to see through the fictions of ego and separation that seem to engulf humanity. At their most benevolent, these psychedelics could offer a direct experience of coexistence with all things and help to open one's heart to the mystery of life itself.

As people experimented with the psychedelic substances, they began to realize that Daoists, Hindus, and Buddhists were already quite well-versed in feelings of oceanic oneness and compassion, and people found that visionary drug experiences were often best explained by Eastern spiritual texts. Timothy Leary and Richard Alpert advised using *The Tibetan Book of the Dead* and the *Tao Te Ching* for guidance during LSD sessions, and many people came to understand that what they were experiencing on LSD was not just hallucinatory play but a mystical perception of reality.

It is a truism that drugs were a central part of the 1960s counterculture, and many of us indulged freely. Just as people used to say that they only drank alcohol for medicinal purposes, I could try to claim that I only took LSD and marijuana to expand my consciousness. If my memory serves me at all, however, I mostly chose to get high for the existential kick, the sense of being present and fully alive in each moment, a feeling I would later pursue through meditation. Drug experiences amplified my idealism, fueling images of personal and social transformation. In fact, at the time, I think my friends and I saw our use of LSD and marijuana as part of the solution. We did not imagine that drugs would burn up so many lives in the years to come. We seemed to be under the protection of good shamanic spirits, and many of us now wonder why they left us.

. . .

The Bay Area counterculture of the late sixties and early seventies was a cauldron of experimentation, often a mixture of drugs with some kind of political or spiritual fervor. The combinations produced some bizarre stories.

For example, on the very day that American astronauts first stepped on the moon, a young hippie in San Francisco took LSD and jumped off the Golden Gate Bridge. He survived the leap, and a day later I went to interview him in his hospital room. He told me that he had jumped "for spiritual advancement" and said that it didn't hurt when he hit the water because he simply left his body until the impact was over.

I later spliced the hippie's words together with Neil Armstrong's historic transmission from the moon, making a tape loop of the two voices that said, "I jumped off the bridge for spiritual advancement…. It's one giant leap for mankind." Beneath that statement, the Byrds were singing "Eight Miles High."

Another story that captures that era for me took place in 1969 during a struggle over People's Park in Berkeley. In the summer of that year, word leaked out that the

University of California was going to put a parking lot on a vacant square of land adjacent to the counterculture enclave of Telegraph Avenue. Local hippies and radicals decided they wanted to preserve this bit of nature, so they planted a garden, set up benches, and began calling it People's Park. Although no one realized it at the time, this was one of the early skirmishes of the environmental movement.

The battle over People's Park had all the elements of mythic theater. The protesters were defying the automobile, the icon of industrial America, in order to protect a piece of nature in the heart of a city. Urban planners now acknowledge the need for open space, and environmental organizations are dedicated to preserving it, but back then it was simply flowers versus concrete, an instinctive reaction to the onslaught of progress. We would stop them here, reversing the trend chronicled by Joni Mitchell: "They paved paradise, put up a parking lot. O-o-o-o-w, bop bop bop bop."

The People's Park protests led to full-fledged battle, which escalated into troop carriers on the respectable streets of Berkeley and tear gas in the air over the prestigious campus. Governor Ronald Reagan finally decided to call out National Guard troops, who put a fence up around the park and stationed men with rifles, bayonets at the ready, to defend it. A few of the Guardsmen's rifles usually had flowers sticking out of the barrels, put there by hippies to create the perfect symbol of the clashing cultures.

One day during the People's Park riots, I was hanging out on a street corner with my tape recorder and met three excited, long-haired radicals who were preparing for an afternoon of skirmishes with the police. They were wearing football helmets to protect their heads and gloves to protect their hands in case they needed to lob tear gas canisters back at the police. Then, as I watched, they each ceremoniously swallowed a tab of blotter acid, shared a group hug, and then headed off for their afternoon street battle. This scene may have summed up the American youth revolution of the 1960s—taking LSD and trying to save a piece of the planet. While the People's Park riots were going on, I managed to get hold of John Lennon by phone from KSAN. He was in Toronto with Yoko Ono, spending a few days "in bed for peace." Live on the air, I asked John if he had any messages for the people who were trying to protect People's Park, and he replied, "Tell them all to be peaceful. We don't want any fightin' going on at People's Park."

The Berkeley leftists did not like this message, and after the broadcast I was invited to a political consciousness-raising meeting where people were critical of Lennon for being a pacifist—and of me as well, for not trying to convince him of the need for confrontation. But I knew that the Beatles were really a hippie band and not so political. "All you need is love, ya da da da daI.." Besides, as a hippie, I believed in nonviolence. Our tactics were pranks and wordplays and taunts at the system that would get the media's attention. Hippies were into street theater, not street fighting.

. . .

Just as the People's Park riots were winding down, acid guru Timothy Leary brought his own brand of theater to town, announcing that he was entering the race for governor of California against Ronald Reagan. Leary was primarily interested in exploring consciousness through psychedelic drugs, but he could not resist the opportunity to play the prankster-shaman role in the escalating conflict between the establishment and youth culture.

Leary agreed to make his first platform statement on KSAN, and I went over to Berkeley, where he was staying, to bring him over to the city. As we drove across the Bay Bridge, Leary took some LSD and offered me a tab. I could not turn down an opportunity to trip with the high priest, and by the time we reached the KSAN studios the acid was coming on. I couldn't have delivered two coherent sentences in a row, but Leary took the microphone and calmly announced his gubernatorial candidacy, as follows:

> Nine score and thirteen years ago, our bearded visionary forefathers brought forth on this continent a new nation, conceived in joyous revolution, sparked by the Boston Tea Party, and dedicated to the proposition that we are here to be free and to turn on. I think they called it

pursuit of happiness in those days. Berkeley is now a great battlefield of a civil war which rages in this country between the turned-on young and the uptight older generation. We are going to start a new political party to continue this celebration, and we are calling it "the grass roots party." I have faith that the children of the state of California will elect me to the highest office in this state. Let everybody come together and join the party.[6]

Ronald Reagan was reelected governor, and Timothy Leary's percentage of the vote was negligible, perhaps because his constituency was too stoned to go to the polls. It is impossible to even hallucinate what might have happened if Leary had won.

. . .

Looking back over underground newspapers from the late 1960s, I am often embarrassed by the overblown political rhetoric of my hippie and radical friends, including some wild statements of my own. I still have a 1969 issue of the *Dock of the Bay,* a short-lived San Francisco alternative newspaper that features a picture of me as KSAN news director mugging a maniacal look as I tear wire copy out of a United Press International teletype machine and drape it around my neck. The caption under the picture quotes me as saying, "The KSAN news department is part of the revolution." It feels so embarrassing to read that now, maybe because whatever revolution I had in mind at the time seems to have failed, miserably. However, I don't feel so bad about my own bombast when I remember the text on the back cover of Jerry Rubin's book *Do It! Scenarios of the Revolution,* which claims, "Jerry Rubin has written the *Communist Manifesto* of our era ... comparable to Che Guevara's *Guerrilla Warfare.*" What were we thinking?

Speaking of Che Guevara, in the fall of 1969, I was asked to appear with two other journalists from the alternative press on William F. Buckley's national TV show *Firing Line,* and for the occasion I wore a Che Guevara T-shirt and brought along a water pistol. Buckley demolished us with his debating skills, and toward the end of the show I finally fired the squirt gun at him. Alas, he was out of range, and I ended up shooting myself in the foot.

Of course my parents were watching the show. My appearance on *Firing Line* was even announced on the front page of the hometown newspaper, the *Norfolk Daily News.* Later my mother told me that the townspeople had been very excited, stopping by my parents' shoe store on the day of the show to congratulate them in advance. The day after the show aired, however, not wanting to embarrass them further, the citizens of Norfolk didn't mention a word to my parents about having seen it.

. . .

At the core of the rebellions of the sixties and seventies was a naive spiritual yearning for a new world and new consciousness. Perhaps the vision is best summarized in a flyer that was handed out at the 1967 antiwar march on the Pentagon. The protesters claimed to be performing an exorcism and announced that they would try to physically levitate the Pentagon itself. Their flyer wove together an antiwar statement with a call for a grand communion of all human cultures in peace and love:

> October 21,1967, Washington, D.C., U.S.A., Planet Earth. We Freemen, of all colors of the spectrum, in the name of God, Ra, Anubis, Osiris, Tlaloc, Quetzalcoatl, Thoth, Chukwu, Olisa-Bulu-Uwa, Imales, Orisasu, Odudua, Kali, Shiva- Shakti, Great Spirit, Dionysus, Yahweh, Thor, Bacchus, Isis, Jesus Christ, Maitreya Buddha, and Rama, do exorcise and cast out the EVIL which has walled and captured the pentacle of power and perverted its use to the need of the total machine and its child the hydrogen bomb and has suffered the people of the planet, earth, the American people and creatures of the mountains, woods, streams, and oceans grievous mental and physical torture and the constant torment of the imminent threat of utter destruction. We are demanding that the pentacle of power once again be used to serve the interests of God manifest in the world as mankind. We are embarking on a motion which is millennial in scope. Let this day, October 21, 1967, mark the beginning of

> suprapolitics. By act of reading this paper you
> are engaged in the Holy Ritual of Exorcism. To
> further participate, focus your thought on the
> casting out of evil through the grace of GOD
> which is all (ours). A billion stars in a billion
> galaxies of space and time is the form of your
> power, and limitless is your name.[7]

The protesters surrounded the Pentagon on that day and chanted *Om* in their attempt to levitate the building. And it worked! At least according to a few very unreliable sources.

. . .

Although radicals and hippies joined together to protest the war in Vietnam, there was always some tension between the two groups. Radicals often accused hippies of being self-indulgent mystics, while hippies accused radicals of being stuck in outdated political forms. The psychospiritual explorers had a somewhat different agenda than did the political left.

One bizarre incident serves to illustrate the rift. In 1976 a group of radicals in New York distributed a leaflet accusing the Dalai Lama of murdering Chairman Mao. The Dalai Lama indeed had performed a special Tibetan Buddhist ritual, the Kalachakra, on the very day that Mao died, and when the leftists heard about it, they decided to blame the ritual for Mao's death. But some Americans who had been studying Tibetan Buddhism quickly intervened. They called a press conference to announce that since Mao had died on the same day as the Kalachakra ceremony, he would be assured passage to Buddha heaven. In other words, not only had the Dalai Lama not murdered Chairman Mao, but he also may even have saved him a few million reincarnations. According to the Buddhists, the Maoists had been both politically and spiritually incorrect.

.   .   .

In some ways the boomer hippies and radicals were exactly who the rest of America thought we were: a bunch of delinquents on an extended tantrum. We were mad at the world for not being the paradise we had been promised by our parents and the Advertising Council. Remember, we didn't have goals, we had "demands." We wanted the world, and we wanted it—then!

In other ways, I believe that our instincts were good and our understanding sound. The United States had become a nation devoted to its own comforts, blind to its exploitation of other peoples and the destruction of the natural world. We challenged our society and its citizens to change their ways, and we put up a thin line of resistance. Too bad we weren't taken more seriously, but that is partly because we insisted on combining our protests with music and revelry. We were just drawing on the honorable tradition of the jesters, who have always worn colorful clothing and challenged the authorities with pranks and street theater.

At the very least, the hippies did help to bring an end to the war in Vietnam and also helped to launch the New Age spiritual movement and the modern environmental movement, and for all of those reasons, I think there should be a statue of the "unknown hippie" placed on the mall in Washington, DC. People could visit the memorial and give the peace sign, and maybe leave behind notes, joints, and old political buttons.

8

OUTWARD MOBILITY

> *"It was my destiny to join in a great experience.*
> *Our goal was not only the East, or rather the East*
> *was not only a country and something geograph-*
> *ical, but it was the home and youth of the soul,*
> *it was everywhere and nowhere, it was the union*
> *of all times."*
>
> —HERMAN HESSE, *The Journey to the East*

ONE OF THE privileges of growing up just as America became a superpower was that many of its middle-class citizens were given the leisure and means to travel all over the world. It was during those midcentury journeys that America's children began gathering the beliefs, symbols, and stories of many other cultures and bringing them home to add to our mythological stew.

Whereas the lost generation of American expatriates went to Europe and North Africa to feed their artistic ambitions or to experiment with socialist ideals, many of the boomers went farther East, seeking to raise consciousness. Hemingway went to cover the Spanish Civil War; we charged off to do battle with the fascist powers of conditioned response and ego domination. Orwell was down and out in London and Paris; we stayed in vermin-infested hotels in Kolkata and Kathmandu on our way to ultimate liberation.

Of course, some Westerners had discovered Buddhist dharma or Hindu Vedanta long before we did. Many British intellectuals who lived in or visited their country's imperial outposts became fascinated with Chinese and Indian religious traditions. The British, however, with a few notable exceptions, saw Eastern spiritual practices as little more than curiosities to be written up in travel books or anthropological papers. Remember that the British controlled the Asian spice trade for centuries without ever learning how to use those spices in their own cooking, and when it came to Eastern wisdom the British never learned how, as the yogis say, to "cook themselves."

In 1970, I joined thousands of young Westerners who were traveling to Asia in what turned out to be a pilgrimage of historic proportions. Some were just seeking thrills, often in the form of cheap and plentiful Asian drugs and exotic venues in which to take them, but many were on their way to do the full-circle spiritual tour, from the Himalayan caves to the South Indian Theosophical Society. Many of us saw the Indian subcontinent as a new holy land, and we were on a quest for the grail of cosmic truths, a guru (mother, father) we could call our own, or a spiritual balm that could soothe our addled postmodern hearts and minds.

My motives were mixed. I was happy to be on an exotic road adventure, but I also wanted to find someone to give me those "being" lessons. After all the books I had read about the Asian wisdom schools, I was eager to begin emptying my mind, creating a brand-new me that was filled with ease, self-acceptance, and maybe even bliss. I was hot on the trail of transformation.

I felt a little guilty leaving the United States during the antiwar struggle, and I remember trying to explain to some of my radical friends that what I was seeking in Asia was an important part of the revolution. But the goal was vague in my own mind, and often during my travels I felt like a self-indulgent imperialist, taking advantage of my privileged birth to seek personal happiness.

. . .

In the late sixties and early seventies, most Western seekers traveled to the East on a route that became known as the hashish trail. This series of bumpy highways started anywhere in Europe and wound across Turkey, where many were long detained for some hassle or another, and then through the deserts of Iran and Afghanistan, still passable at that time, where travelers often lingered for some hashish-dream days wandering the narrow streets of Kabul in search of a trippy looking mosque.

The hashish trail soon became littered with strung-out, destitute young people, some sick with amebic dysentery or hepatitis, many half insane from culture shock, their illness and disorientation amplified by Afghani and

Kashmiri hashish, Thai stick, psilocybin mushrooms, or the high-grade Pakistani and Chinese opium and heroin.

Eventually, some concerned Westerners organized ways to help this traveling Haight-Ashbury of the East. In Kathmandu, for instance, a few people created an informal travelers' aid center in a restaurant called the Bakery. If you were lost, broke, addicted, or just wanted information about a good ashram, the people at the Bakery could help. They offered yoga and meditation classes, free food and warm clothing, and sometimes even money to get back to the West.

A multitude of bizarre and amazing tales arose from the hippie migration to the East. A notable one is of Michael Riggs, a very tall (6'4") San Diego surfer who headed off to Europe in 1966 and eventually found himself hanging out in Greece with a Russian princess named Zena. They traveled to India, where Zena went her own way after deciding that she was the reincarnation of the nineteenth-century spiritualist Madame Blavatsky. Michael Riggs, meanwhile, became an Indian sadhu through and through. He wrapped a single cloth, a *longi,* around his body, matted his long curly hair with ashes, and began wandering barefoot around India from holy place to holy place, singing Hindu devotional songs and playing an *ektar,* a one-stringed instrument. Michael Riggs, the surfer from San Diego, was eventually given the name Bhagavan Das by his guru, Neem Karoli Baba, and later became famous for leading psychologist Richard Alpert to this very same teacher. Soon thereafter, Richard Alpert became Baba Ram Dass and went back to America to write *Be Here Now,* a book that washed another, even bigger, wave of Western seekers onto the shores of cosmic India.

. . .

It was a lark for us to live on the cheap, and it became a kind of contest to see who could stay in Asia the longest time on the least amount of money. The competition was tough. I knew people who came to India or Nepal with just a few hundred dollars and stayed for years. They begged and scrounged, they sold their passports or pulled some lost-traveler's-check scam, they went from ashram to ashram and temple to temple living off the *prasad* (holy offerings). One couple who did Buddhist meditation retreats with me made money to stay on in India by smuggling Buddha statues filled with hashish back to the West.

Many of the young Western pilgrims to Asia seemed to be very good at adopting a new identity, and some got a good start on their inner transformation by taking on a new name and a new wardrobe. Those who stayed for any length of time almost always began to adopt the local dress, replacing shirts and pants with various pieces of cloth. In India and Southeast Asia, much of the traditional clothing does not have buttons or zippers, snaps or belts, and when you get up in the morning you don't get dressed, you get wrapped.

My friends and I eventually accumulated many different pieces of fabric of all shapes and sizes: *dhotis*, *longis*, sarongs, shawls, scarves, and so on. Each piece has a specific function, hut often I would see Westerners wearing something around their head that was meant for their waist or vice versa. It's all just cloth, anyway. Wind it around your neck, midriff, and loins, and you were wrapped for the day!

. . .

As on all spiritual journeys, we had to confront the dark forces, and in India that often came in the form of amebic dysentery. The subcontinent's bugs seemed to love the fat blood of Westerners, and almost everyone who spent more than a few months in India or Nepal eventually came down with some wretched disease (pun intended).

Once in Dharamsala, India, after feeling slightly feverish and listless for a few days, I visited the local Tibetan medical clinic, called the Tibetan Medical and Astro Institute. I explained my symptoms to a sweet Tibetan woman, who breastfed her baby while diagnosing my condition. She then handed me several sheets of paper describing various Tibetan pills that I might want to try. One was the *Chakril Chenmo*, or Great Iron Pill, touted as a blood purifier and excellent for sluggishness and fevers as well as all eye ailments. This wonder pill consists of forty different ingredients, including "purified iron filings, three myrobalans without seeds, Kashmiri saffron, musk, solidified bile of elephant, saxifraga pasumensis marg, purified magnetic stone, adhatoda vasica, sea shells, white and red sandalwood, meconopsis species, costus roots, Indian valerian, rhino horn, and asphaltum." The solidified bile of elephant didn't bother me as much as "asphaltum," which I guessed was ground-up pieces of highway. Most such Tibetan pills come with the instructions "If possible, one should recite the mantra of the medicine Buddha, *Tadyatha aum bhaishjya maha bhaihjya raja samud gate svaha,* and the mantra of Avalokitesvara, *Aum mani padme hum,* as many times as possible before taking the pill."

What finally cured me of my ailment, I believe, was lots of Nepali chicken soup. Joseph Campbell may have found common myths throughout the world, but an equally important discovery is the universal sanctity of chicken soup. From an early age I was fed chicken soup as the Jewish cure for all kinds of *tzuris,* from flu to depression, but I never suspected that, in fact, chicken soup is a balm of equal importance throughout the world. Everywhere on the planet, people are cooking chicken soups. With regional ingredients added— sambal and rice in Indonesia; cilantro and noodles in Nepal; curry and rice in India; lime, chiles, and potatoes in Mexico and Guatemala; wontons, noodles, and chiles in China and Thailand; matzo balls, celery, and carrots in New York—chicken soups offer the requisite nutrients for psychic as well as physical healing.

While many of us were in India to find cosmic consciousness, we might have gained some historical perspective as well. Strewn across the Indian landscape are the bricks and bones of several old empires, a constant reminder of the impermanence of worldly wealth and power, something we don't encounter much in America.

Once when I was stuck in New Delhi waiting for a plane back to the States, I went out for a few holes of golf at the Delhi Golf Club with some friends. On one hole my ball landed on what I thought was a bunch of old bricks and rocks, and I asked my caddie if I could move it back onto the grass. "Yes, of course," he said. "These Mogul ruins are not a natural hazard." My ball was lying in the middle of a four-hundred-year-old archaeological site!

The Western pilgrims to the Indian subcontinent followed a regular circuit, usually dictated by the seasons. Many spent their winters in the plains of India, visiting gurus and studying in ashrams and retreat centers. By March, when it started getting too hot, they would make their way up toward the Himalayas, either to Nepal or to the Indian hill stations, where they could spend the summer hanging out with the sweet mountain people, trekking, or maybe studying in a Tibetan Buddhist monastery. In the fall, people would head back down to the plains again and, finally, to the yearly Christmas bash on the golden beaches of Goa, where many hundreds of Western travelers would gather to dance, take drugs, and exchange mystical practices and tales of their Asian adventures.

Another part of the travelers' circuit led through Southeast Asia. Indian visas lasted for only three months, and unless you could find a good excuse to get an extension, you would have to leave India for a while before being allowed to return. While some people would conveniently lose their passports or simply risk getting caught with an outdated visa in order to remain in India, many travelers headed farther east for a few months.

A common odyssey was to fly or boat to Thailand, journey by train down through Malaysia to Singapore, take a boat across the South China Sea to Jakarta and a train across Java to Bali, and then reverse directions and make your way back up to India. These trips through Southeast Asia were a chance to recuperate from the diet and diseases of India and Nepal. One could spend time on the beaches of Thailand and Malaysia and Indonesia, swimming in the warm ocean to wash off accumulated grime, eating seafood and fruit to gain strength for yet another stint chasing enlightenment on the subcontinent.

When we gathered at the travelers' hotels in Singapore or Bangkok, we would trade stories of our adventures. My contribution was usually a story about the time I rode all night through the jungles of Sumatra on a bus jammed with peasants and their animals. What made this trip peculiar was that the bus driver drove along singing pop songs into a microphone that had been hooked up over his seat. The singing driver was accompanied by a man who sat next to him and played a small electric organ that was propped up on the dashboard. Most unusual, however, was the fact that a big loudspeaker was mounted on top of the bus, so that as we rode along through the night this live performance went booming out over the jungle. I never could find out if there was a reason for this—maybe it was to warn oncoming traffic or scare away thieves—but I imagined prowling tigers and big-eyed owls astounded by this rambling Sumatran jukebox-bus and the driver's heavily accented voice singing, "r-r-r-ollin', r-r-r-ollin,' r-r-r-ollin' onna rivah."

> *All India is full of holy men stammering gospels in strange tongues; shaken and consumed in the fires of their own zeal; dreamers, babblers, and visionaries: as it has been from the beginning and will continue to the end.*
>
> —RUDYARD KIPLING

My spiritual journey in India began in Varanasi, the holiest city in a nation full of holy cities, the birthplace of Lord Shiva, the Hindu deity who rules over life and death. Varanasi marks the spot where, three thousand years ago, a group of sages sat down on the banks of the Ganges River and began to intuit the size of the cosmos and explain the karma of the universe. The sages who wrote the *Upanishads* lived in Varanasi, and later the Buddha himself came to a nearby forest to "turn the wheel of the *dharma*" and begin his teachings.

So I consider it auspicious that I received my first Asian spiritual teaching in Varanasi, on the banks of the holy Ganges River. As a hippie seeker, I also find it appropriate to have been given my Indian initiation by a hashish-smoking "Shiva baba." Considered to be one of the world's oldest religious cults, the Shiva babas number in the millions in India. They are mendicant wanderers, moving from holy place to holy place, continuously praying to Lord Shiva, and sometimes using hashish to amplify their prayers. The Shiva babas were the original hippies.

One of my first days in Varanasi, I was sitting down by the cremation grounds watching the bodies burning when this crazy-looking old man with matted hair wearing only a loincloth, his face streaked with ash marks and painted with red designs, ambled up to me and said, "Hello, my friend, what do you want?" At first I thought he was trying to sell me something, so I shook my head and turned away. But then he said, "Are you looking for something here in India?" I turned and appraised him and finally decided to answer. "Enlightenment. Freedom. That's all."

"Then follow me," he said. And without a look back, he turned and walked down toward the river. After a few minutes I got up and followed him, and by the time I had reached the spot where he was sitting he had already laid out a piece of cloth on the sand, placed a chillum pipe on it, and was busy rubbing a piece of hashish with tobacco to prepare us a smoke.

After I smoked a pipe with this holy fool, I asked him if he could give me any spiritual advice. As soon as he began to speak, I realized that he didn't care whether I became his disciple or not, that he wanted nothing from me but my company over a bowl or two of hashish.

"I will give you one important piece of advice," he said. "No matter what prayers or meditations you are doing, be sure to awaken before the sun comes up. Then you will have a chance to calm and focus your mind after sleeping, before the light of the sun comes to reveal all the world to you and distract you from yourself." I bow down to my Shiva baba for that fine advice. In whatever incarnation he is now, may he have many a nice day.

While Varanasi is the holiest city in India, it is also the center of the Indian silk trade, and thousands of touts and hustlers will surround and bombard you with their sales pitches from the minute you arrive until the minute you leave. In Varanasi the silk trade is second only to the business with the gods.

One morning, when I had nothing else to do, I went into a nicely appointed silk store a bit early, just as the proprietor was arranging his stock for the day's commerce. A handsome middle-aged Indian man in Western pants and blazer, greeted me in fluent English. With his dark brown eyes and black hair, he could have passed for a Jewish businessman in New York or Chicago. In fact, he somewhat resembled my father, right down to his fine manners. I was comforted by the scene's familiarity until I turned around and saw this respectable businessman light a stick of incense and begin praying to a statue of the elephant god Ganesha, which was perched right on top of his cash register. It was one thing to see the wild-looking street people praying to elephant and monkey gods, but to see this prosperous, well-spoken gentleman bowing down before this idol was somehow incongruous and shocking to me. I later told my father this story and showed him a picture of Ganesha. He laughed and laughed. "Imagine," my father said, "praying to an elephant!" I didn't tell him that I was a little jealous of Hinduism's colorful pantheon of deities. The one and only God I grew up with would not let himself be seen, and maybe that's why I had such a hard time finding him.

India was full of gods and gurus, and our biggest problem was that there were so many of both to choose from. Some Westerners came to India to stay at a specific Hindu ashram, perhaps one that had been founded by one of the famous old masters such as Yogananda or Ramakrishna, or one run by a hotshot lineage holder whose fame had spread to the West, like the Beatles' guru, Maharishi Mahesh Yogi, or Ram Dass's guru, Neem Karoli Baba. Others became disciples of more obscure Indian yogis. I met one young woman from Ohio who found her guru living in a tiny wooden box in Varanasi. People in the neighborhood said that this holy man had not spoken in thirty years, so this fresh-faced young Midwestern girl just sat outside the box every day for nearly a year, content to be near him and "feel his presence." A young man I knew from upstate New York moved into a Himalayan cave in order to be near his wild mountain guru. He stayed for almost six months, until one night both of them were chased away by a tiger.

I did some guru shopping, checking out various spiritual scenes. I had interviewed a yogi named Swami Satchidananda on the radio in San Francisco, and he told me that I looked just like Satya Sai Baba—especially because of my wild, kinky hair—and said that if I ever got to India I must go visit this holy man. Satya Sai Baba was considered an incarnated deity by millions of people in southern India and was said to be able to materialize objects out of thin air. I tried to track him down at his various ashrams but kept missing him. As a consolation, his disciples smeared my forehead with some ashes that he had supposedly materialized.

I visited Bhagwan Sri Rajneesh at his ashram in Poona, and since this was before his rise to fame, I easily gained an audience with him. Rajneesh had me try one of his "chaotic meditations," encouraging me to twirl around and around as fast as possible, all the while shouting, "Who? Who? Who?" After a half-hour of dizzying hyperventilation and self-questioning, I was told to fall to the floor and lie there quietly listening for the answer. All I ever got was silence and a little nausea, which may indeed be the answer.

Swami Muktananda was one of the heavies, the Hindu equivalent of a hip Catholic cardinal in a big American diocese, a guru with real power and lineage behind him. Muktananda was a spiritual guide to some of Bombay's wealthiest Indians, counting among his admirers none other than Indian prime minister Indira Gandhi. I was fortunate enough to drive up to his ashram just after sunset and got a good view of the huge neon *Om* sign that was visible for several miles around.

Despite the cabaret-like sign, inside Muktananda's ashram I felt an unmistakable vibration, a tangible atmosphere of peace and purity common to many of India's monasteries and holy places. Sai Baba's ashrams and Neem Karoli Baba's temples had the same quality, possibly the effect of years of incessant prayer and meditation. The feeling of sanctuary that these places provided may also have had something to do with the contrast between the cleanliness and calm found within them and the chaos of India just outside their doors.

As my friends and I traveled around the spiritual circuit, we kept hearing about this or that teacher who had a shortcut to enlightenment or who specialized in teaching Westerners or had miraculous powers. It seemed that on every Himalayan peak and in every ashram on the Deccan plain another guru was offering a better bliss and an emptier emptiness. Meanwhile, many young Westerners, always on the lookout for the ultimate exotic experience, became fascinated by tales of certain yogis who practiced the mysterious tantric arts.

Tantra is an esoteric school of yoga and meditation that tries to harness all human energies in the service of higher consciousness. Tantric masters have developed various rituals and exercises that will stir up our deepest desires and fears, so that we can then practice overcoming and transforming them. For example, students of Tantra are often instructed to meditate among the corpses at cremation grounds, contemplating their own death. After a while, the Yogi becomes more comfortable with his or her inevitable fate and the emotions that surround it.

Since sex is one of the most powerful human drives, the tantric masters have developed special techniques to work with sexual energy. In tantric sex one prolongs intercourse by deepening the breath and coordinating it with one's partner, eventually blending the male and female energies until there is no longer any sense of self and other. After an extended period of practice, the couple ostensibly arrives at the unified state of consciousness that existed before the separation of yin and yang, which is to say, before creation itself.

There is no climax in the tantric sexual union, no orgasm or ejaculation. Instead, all energy generated in the genital region gets channeled to the higher centers, or chakras. The way I once heard it described was that male tantric adepts would reverse their ejaculate and drive it up their spines, to literally blow their minds.

Westerners loved stories about the tantric masters. I remember listening to some people who had come down from a remote Tibetan ashram in Sikkim with tales of yogis who had so much control over their genital muscles that they could suck milk up into their bodies through their penises. Their female consorts were said to be able to play the trumpet with their vaginas. Some hippies thought these were fun-sounding things to do, not realizing that such powers are the product of years of rigorous training and renunciation. Many of us were drawn to Tantra by the possibility of prolonged sexual pleasure, but we eventually—a little grudgingly—came to understand that Tantra is about the end of personal pleasure. In fact, it's about the end of personal anything.

· · ·

I attended my first meditation retreat in 1970 at a funky Buddhist temple in Bodhgaya, India, just a few blocks away from where the Buddha had become enlightened 2,500 years earlier. The teacher was a jolly, rotund man named S. N. Goenka, who was traveling through India offering ten-day meditation courses that were attended mostly by Western seekers. On the travelers' circuit, people had dubbed Goenka the "singing guru" because of the deep, beautiful baritone in which he chanted the Buddhist sutras every morning and evening during his retreats.

Goenka had been a wealthy Indian businessman living in Rangoon, Burma. His family and his business colleagues say he was something of a tyrant and prone to fits of anger. He was also tortured by migraine headaches and had traveled to the best medical clinics in London and Switzerland, searching in vain for a cure. Finally, Goenka met a Buddhist teacher living just a few blocks from him in Rangoon and soon found that meditation helped bring an end to both his headaches and his temper. He was so grateful that he decided to devote his life to teaching others.

Goenka taught a Buddhist practice called Vipassana, or insight meditation, which was said to be a relatively accessible, no-frills path to liberation. Although we signed up to meditate for ten days with Goenka, some of us ended up staying a month, doing three retreats one after the other. After each night's final meditation session, we would gather in the hall or in somebody's hut and talk about what we were learning and how it related to Western psychology and philosophy or to our lives back home.

We were learning a meditation technique that involved scanning the mind up and down the body, from head to toe and back again, in a rhythmic and repetitive manner, focusing on bodily sensations. Goenka called this process "sweeping." We laughed about the possibility of eventually sweeping ourselves out of existence. We were all excited by the notion of getting rid of our egos.

Those who came to sit with the singing guru in Bodhgaya included Ram Dass and a few of his entourage: Joseph Goldstein and Sharon Salzberg, who later became meditation teachers and cofounders of a Buddhist center in the United States; Daniel Goleman, who became the *New York Times* behavioral sciences editor and authored the bestselling book *Emotional Intelligence;* Tsultrim Allione, who wrote a groundbreaking book on women's spirituality; and many others who eventually became teachers and translators, smuggling the true treasures of the East back home with them. This gathering was a significant part of the beginnings of the mindfulness movement.

After the Bodhgaya meditation retreats were over, Ram Dass hired a bus to take people to visit his Hindu teacher, Maharaj-ji, and, although I was invited to go along, I embarked on my futile search for Satya Sai Baba instead. That busload of seekers got to hang out with Maharaj-ji for a while, and eventually he gave them all spiritual names. Linda Thurston became Mirabai,

Sandy Miller became Tara, Danny Goleman became Jaggernath Dass, Jeffery Miller became Surya Das, Jim Litton became Rameshwar Das, and so on. The suffix *dass* in Hindi means "servant of," so Ram Dass is literally the "servant of Ram."

I must say I was rather jealous of the people who got on that bus, and eventually I decided to make up my own spiritual name. I started calling myself "What's Up Dass," the "servant of what's up." It's a good name for both a meditator and a journalist.

Perhaps the fact that I missed both Satya Sai Baba and Neem Karoli Maharaj-ji was the universe's way of keeping me on the Buddha's path. During my time in India I studied with some Hindu teachers, and I was enchanted by the Hindu pantheon of deities, each in its own archetypal display with magical powers and animal allies. But I couldn't pray to them. Maybe the old Jewish commandment against idolatry was still working on me, along with my sense that God either did not take any worldly form or else was present in all forms, in everything.

. . .

Hippies were well acquainted with the idea of the mystical Oneness, either as a notion picked up from modern physics or a vision experienced on drugs. In the sixties, you would often hear someone say, usually in stoned conversation, "Well, everything is everything." That phrase was a conversation stopper for sure: if everything is everything, then no further distinctions are possible and all talk ceases. But the phrase reflected at least a cursory understanding among the hippies that all things are, indeed, connected.

I had gone to India with a vague notion that I would find a guru who would teach me how to feel at one with everything, to merge with the cosmic Oneness. I assumed that my painful self-consciousness would then disappear, nirvana would kick in, and the bliss would begin. I figured it would take, at the most, maybe a few months.

After five decades of meditation practice, I realize that merging with the cosmic Oneness is extremely difficult, partly because it is a paradoxical project. First of all, this cosmic Oneness is where we are already. So trying to become one with the One is like playing musical chairs with yourself. But, in spite of the fact that there is really nowhere to go, you've still got to make some effort or you will never remember that you are already there. But the moment you realize that you *are* there, then you aren't there. "You" have disappeared into the Oneness, which may indeed be blissful, but nobody is around to enjoy it.

Most mystics agree that the cosmic Oneness is indescribable, but over the centuries it has been given many different names: the Dao, the Dharma, the Source, the Way, the Great Perfection, Essential Nature. Some call it "the unnameable," a wonderful name.

If you are considering a journey into the One, my advice is to first decide what you want to call it, just in case you get lost and need to ask directions. Jack

Kerouac wrote, "I call it the golden eternity but you can call it anything you want." I have become fond of the Zen word "suchness," which has a funky, down-home kind of ring to it. "I'm just going out on the front porch for a spell, folks, to sit around in the good ol' suchness." Another good Zen name for the cosmic Oneness is "the isness." When confronted with any surprising circumstances, you can then say to yourself, "That's just the business of the isness."

The Tibetan Vajrayana Buddhists have some fantastic names for the mystic Oneness, often expressed in dohas, spontaneous poems of awakening. Names for the Oneness found in these poems include the Predicateless Primordial Essence; the Transcendent Fullness of the Emptiness (have yourself a waltz with that paradox); the Dissolver of Space and Time; the Weaver of the Web of Appearances; and, last but not least, the Outbreather and the Inbreather of Infinite Universes Throughout the Endlessness of Duration.

I notice that modern physics has also given us a few new names for the Oneness, such as "the space-time continuum." That name could also be used as a mantra, if you just hold the "… uum."

I often refer to the cosmic Oneness as "the big everything," or else "the big nothing," depending on my mood. But it is difficult to establish any feeling for abstractions such as these and almost impossible to worship them. That's why most people give the Oneness a face and personality. They want their metaphysics to be user-friendly. Enter the gods and goddesses.

Humans like having a personal creator to adorn and adore or even to curse and beseech. Brahma, Isis, Allah, Jehovah—these are the agents we have chosen to represent the Oneness for us. Each of them might be viewed as a stand-in or stuntperson for the big everything. It is interesting to note that most of our gods and goddesses end up looking somewhat like ourselves: as the Preacher in Ecclesiastes says, "All is vanity."

Unfortunately, people are always claiming to have found the exclusive name for the cosmic Oneness, and many have fought wars, slaughtered, enslaved, and tortured others, all because they had different names for the supreme being. Sometimes people even kill each other in the name of the *very same* god, which must make it hard for the deity in question to take sides. I can imagine that someday the true god or goddess will come down from the heavens and announce to humanity, "You all got my name wrong."

Many of the boomer spiritual seekers grew up alienated from all that god business and so instead turned to the bare, a-mythical essence of everything. By rejecting all the agents, or at least putting them on hold, we started exploring ways to have a direct, "unmediated," experience of ultimate reality. Typical of our generation, we said, "No more secondhand gods! No more worn-out metaphors! We want the Oneness, and we want it now!"

9

INWARD MOBILITY

We have seen idols elephantine-snouted,
And thrones with living gems bestarred and pearled,
And palaces whose riches would have routed
The dreams of all the bankers in the world.
We have seen wonder-striking robes and dresses,
Women whose nails and teeth the betel stains
And jugglers whom the rearing snake caresses.
What then? What then?

—CHARLES BAUDELAIRE

MY FIRST MEDITATION retreat remains the most shocking experience of my life. Nobody in my culture had told me that I could actually step out of my own drama and then turn my attention around to observe myself. When I began this process of self-observation I was completely unprepared for what I saw.

Goenka's first instructions were very simple. "Just pay attention to your breath," he said. "Don't do anything else. Just feel your breath going in and out."

I was able to stay focused for two or three breaths, and then I noticed that my mind was continuing to think. It was generating thoughts all by itself! And when the content of a thought seemed important or interesting enough (Do I have enough money to stay in India for another few months? When can I possibly have sex again?), my mind would become completely absorbed in the subject matter and begin planning, fantasizing, or remembering—whatever was called for—so that eventually I lost all awareness of my breath. And when I finally did notice that I was "lost in thought," another voice would usually appear in my mind and begin criticizing me for not being able to stay focused. "You idiot. Why can't you just stay with your breath? You don't do anything right!"

How could this be? My mind was arguing with itself! First it had disobeyed my wishes, distracting me from my breath, and then it had the gall to accuse me of intentionally becoming distracted! How strange it was to listen to these different voices in my head, jabbering on and on, and none of them ever consulting with *me*.

Fascinated and disturbed, I drew on my journalistic skills and tried to record my mental babble. Journalists are trained to be objective, dispassionate observers, just like meditators, but in meditation the story being covered is oneself and that makes objectivity much more difficult. Nonetheless, I was able to capture a little of what it sounded like inside my mind during that first meditation retreat, and, swallowing my pride, I offer a few minutes of the transcription. Take my mind, please:

> Ahhh, inbreath-outbreath.... I'm resolved to stay focused on my breath this hour ... inbreath ... I'll just move my knee over a little ... there.... Oh no, that position is going to make my leg sore before too long.... I'll just move it back over here.... I hope nobody was looking.... Okay, outbreath.... Maybe I should count my breaths for a while until my mind gets settled.... Inbreath one... outbreath ... inbreath two ... outbreath ... If I get up to twenty I'll start over.... Inbreath three ... whoa, did I miss one breath? I can't remember.... Okay, I'll start over with inbreath one again ... darn.... Darn? ... Did I just judge myself for losing count? ... I shouldn't be judging myself so much.... Okay, outbreath.... But wait, I just judged myself for judging myself! What a mess these synapses are! ... Luckily it's not my essential self, whatever the hell that is.... Okay, now back to the breath.... Concentrate! Why is this so hard? Everybody else seems to be doing okay.... Whoops, I'm supposed to keep my eyes closed.... "Living is easy with eyes closed." The Beatles weren't doing this damn meditation technique when they wrote that song.... And why am I always humming something? My mind has been destroyed by rock and roll.... Damn, another

self-judgment!... Okay, back to the task ...
inbreath one ... outbreath ... inbreath two....

Tibetan Buddhist master Chögyam Trungpa once
said, "The spiritual path is insult after insult," and that
became clearer as I continued to meditate. What I found
most disturbing, even embarrassing, especially during
those first few meditation retreats, was that my mind so
often insisted on singing to me. I would be sitting there
meditating, and suddenly, triggered by a random image
or thought, a song would start up and begin playing over
and over again inside my head. Other meditators have
reported similar musical intrusions, which might be
called "jukebox karma."

Often I could stay aware of my breath and yet still
hear a song playing faintly in the background of my
mind, as if some inner DJ was trying to offer me some
music to meditate by. But instead of New Age meditation music, I was getting pop songs, the ones with strong
hooks, such as, "Rollin' on a river..." or "We all live in a
yellow submarine...." I would try my hardest to turn off
the songs, but, like an irritating drunk singing out in the
street, my mind refused to stop.

Sometimes, mercifully, the song that arose in my
head was one that appeared on an album side that was
familiar to me. Then at least I would get some variety in
my mental playlist—as my mind tracked through the rest
of the songs on the album side! Sometimes it would even
flip the album over and play through the second side.
"Good day, sunshine ..." These pop songs were little

sutras about the personal dramas of life, usually about losing, winning, or looking for love.

Seeing the independent, rebellious, nature of one's mind can be especially disturbing to someone from our culture, where we identify so thoroughly with our mind's contents. We not only believe that we generate and control all of our own thoughts, we also have come to believe that those thoughts define us, almost exclusive of anything else. In our culture, heads are us!

What happened as I listened to my mind singing and thinking and running on without me was that I began to doubt that I *was* my mind. I became aware that my mind has a mind of its own.

.   .   .

During those first retreats I had a hard time understanding this new perspective I was gaining on myself, but twenty-five years later my insights were confirmed and explained by neuroscience. *Time* magazine ran a cover story titled "In Search of the Mind," summarizing the latest brain research at the time. Readers of this article may have been surprised to hear that the mind was lost, and they were probably more disturbed to learn that even the neuroscientists couldn't find it.

Now, the latest research concludes that our ordinary, everyday mind is actually the product of evolution's brain, a so-called self-organizing system, which works in a rather perfunctory way to produce our interpretations of the world and to motivate our behaviors. What is most disturbing, however, is that the scientists cannot find any control center in our brain; no authority figure is up there making decisions and pulling the levers. The *Time* article concludes, "Despite our every instinct to the contrary, consciousness is not some entity inside the brain that corresponds to 'self,' some kernel of awareness that runs the s h o w.... After more than a century of looking for it, brain researchers have concluded that such a self simply does not exist."

Whoa! Wait a minute. Actual scientists are now telling us that there is no one inside our heads running the show, telling us that our conscious "self" does not exist? And it's all right there in *Time* magazine almost thirty years ago! Why wasn't there a nationwide or even worldwide panic, with people jumping off tall buildings or going berserk?

Throughout the centuries, practitioners of meditation have realized the deeply conditioned nature of our ordinary mind and the fact that an autonomous self is not necessarily in charge of its functioning. The result is not insanity but instead the beginnings of a new freedom of mind—an increasing ability to doubt, ignore, or even override the habitual, reactive circuits of the brain. Seeing into our own brain-mind is the first step in a lifelong process of "liberation" from our biological and psychological conditioning.

The simultaneous discovery of "no-self" by the scientists and the new crop of Western meditators may have just been a coincidence, but it seems to point to a necessary adjustment of consciousness in our time, a pendulum swing back from the Cartesian belief that I think therefore I am and that I am what I think, along with the excessive individualism that comes from identifying solely with what goes on in one's head.

.   .   .

In those first meditation retreats, I also "got down," as we used to say, and became more intimate with my body. We were acquainted before, certainly, but in meditation I noticed that my body got tired when it wanted, hungry when it wanted, even became sore and itchy when it wanted, without once asking my permission. I began to understand that my body, like my mind, has a life of its own. This might seem like a commonsense understanding, but the repeated, closeup view of this truth in meditation makes it come alive.

I would sit there on my meditation cushion and feel the pulses of breath and heartbeat, the energies coursing through the nervous system, the sounds and sensations registering on consciousness, the muscles contracting and relaxing—and all of it was taking place without me lifting a finger. I began to experience that it all goes on, as George Harrison wrote, "within you and without you."

> *To study Buddhism is to study the self. To study the self is to know the self. To know the self is to forget the self.*
>
> —Zen master Dogen

After a few years of doing meditation practice, I began to see parts of myself dropping away. All aspects of this life that I had considered "I," "me," or "mine" were being called into doubt. I was being confronted with the fundamental question of all esoteric spiritual traditions, the age-old mystic inquiry "Who am I?" Around this question everything revolves, because how we come to view ourselves in the scheme of things will determine how we feel about our lives and the world and even how we treat each other and the environment.

The great sages have posed the Inquiry in many colorful ways. Zen masters might ask, "Who is it that is going in and out through these six sense doors?" or "Who is it that is dragging this corpse (your body) around?" The Hopi say that we must ask ourselves, "What am I?" A Hindu Advaita Vedanta teacher might reply to a disciple's question "Who am I?" by asking, "Who is it that is asking this question?" pushing us back against the wall of our own desire to know. Socrates turned the question into an imperative: "Know thyself."

Meditation practice can be understood as a process of self-investigation, which, after many years, can lead to a degree of self-liberation. It is a process that seemed especially appropriate to many of us Westerners who were living in a cultural era of shifting roles and slippery identities.

But meditation does not make you into someone else. Many people, including me, had some vague notion in the beginning that through meditation we could get rid of our personality or even get ourselves a new one—a personality that we could live with more easily. It turns out, however, that personality is very persistent, like the shape of your ears, and doesn't change that much over time. As an old Spanish proverb says, "Natures and features survive to the grave." What happens through meditation is an ever-increasing realization that we don't create who we are and that our personality is, to a great extent, inherited—genetically, epigenetically, and from the circumstances of our life, especially the early years. After a time, the intense identification we have with ourselves begins to weaken. We find that we don't have to take our personality so personally. Our temperaments and idiosyncrasies no longer define us. As Ram Dass said, "I haven't gotten rid of any of my neuroses, but they no longer have much power over me." Even though the process of meditation can sometimes feel like a disappearing act, the good news is that as you lose yourself you begin to gain the world. From years of meditation practice, I have increasingly experienced myself as interwoven with all of the universe, integrated with the forces of cosmic and biological evolution. It's not a big feeling or any peak experience but rather a more relaxed and sympathetic settling in with who I am. The feelings of alienation have started to heal.

> *"In seeking, you discover that you are neither body nor mind. And the love of the self in you is for the self in all. The two are one. The*

consciousness in you and the consciousness in me, apparently two, really are one ... and they seek their unity. And that is love."

—NISARGADATA MAHARAJ

10

THE NEW AGE

"Start a huge, foolish project, like Noah. It makes absolutely no difference what people think of you."

—JALALUDDIN RUMI

THROUGHOUT THE 1970S, between trips to India, I continued to work at KSAN radio and began covering the then-burgeoning New Age movement. This movement was the bastard child of a beatnik father and a hippie mother, midwifed by renegade Western psychologists and Eastern sages, a multiheaded creature made up of myths and symbols from every corner of the world, all united by the dominant American gene for utopian idealism.

Many of us who became involved in the spiritual traditions of Hinduism or Buddhism tried to deny any association with the New Age or even scorned it as a circus for spiritual dilettantes. But when the Dalai Lama was asked if he was worried that Tibetan Buddhism might be lumped together with New Age spirituality, he replied, "Oh, no. I think we would *all* be happy to have a New Age."

Although I was convinced that Buddhism was my primary spiritual path, I kept sampling from the New Age cornucopia. I tried body therapies, consciousness-raising seminars, personality assessments, health-enhancements, herbal healings, and home appliances.

My motives were mixed, again. Partly, I was searching for perfect moments, another good high. Other times I took part in New Age experiments out of sheer curiosity or for a good news story. And furthermore, I would not have been disappointed to accidentally find a shortcut to nirvana—a special weekend workshop that would give my chakras a spin or tweak my psyche so that I would remain forever at peace.

I tried various body therapies, including both polarity and Rolfing. The idea behind these techniques is that tight muscles hold memories of trauma, and if you can somehow release these blockages and get into alignment, your energy flows more smoothly and you become as mellow as a jellyfish. A couple of the therapists who worked on me seemed to be tearing my muscles and tendons off the bones and shoving them into new positions. I suspect these bodyworkers were the ones who coined the phrase "No pain, no gain."

Boomers had been conditioned to believe that the simple act of buying a new consumer item could bring happiness. Playing to this belief, all sorts of aids and accoutrements were invented to serve the new Western wellness seeker, products that promise to hasten us toward super health, higher consciousness, nirvana, satori, or wherever it is you think you want to go. The Western spirit of commerce could not resist the commerce in spirit. In more recent years, yoga and mindfulness practice themselves have been, in many circles, commodified.

For several years in the 1970s, I had a negative ion generator in my house. Negative ions counteract air pollution and maybe even get rid of bad vibes. Although initially skeptical, I eventually bought one at my local health food store. After trying it out for a few weeks, I went back and told the salesperson that the device didn't seem to make any difference in my mood or general health. The clerk looked me in the eye and said, very sincerely, "Maybe you just aren't sensitive enough to notice the difference." I should have let my anger show, but at the time I was into simply labeling and watching emotions, so I reluctantly took my negative ion generator back home and plugged it in again. After a few years it got tossed into a back closet. I will never know whether those negative ions actually worked or not because there were just too many other variables operating and perhaps I'm just not sensitive enough to notice the difference. It's possible I wouldn't have lived this long if that generator hadn't been filling my living space with negative ions.

For a while I was taking a daily dose of spirulina, a blue-green algae rich in a range of vitamins and minerals. It tasted so terrible I could get it down only by mixing it into shakes and fruit drinks. Perhaps it too has had a curative effect on my life, but all I could realize at the time was getting in touch with my inner fish.

One of my favorite New Age products was a simple massaging device, the Ma-roller, perhaps named after a great mother masseuse goddess. You could give yourself a spinal massage and back rub anytime you wanted by rolling around on your Ma-roller. According to the ads, this wondrous wooden massaging wheel was "designed by a student of Chinese acupuncture who is also a student of yoga ... and is a result of meditations on the five elements as given in the *Huangdi Neijing* (The Yellow Emperor's Classic of Internal Medicine)." I bought it, used it, and loved my Ma-roller.

I also once owned a Footsie-roller, which was kind of a Ma-roller for the soles of your feet. The nerve endings in the feet are connected to all other parts of the body, including internal organs, and massaging those nerve endings just might make you happy as a clam.

Several other devices claim to work on the soles of your feet. If you aren't concerned about using electricity, you can purchase an "electrically heated foot massage roller." And if you are just plain lazy, I assume you can also achieve the benefits of foot massage by wearing—if you can possibly stand it—those little sandals and slippers with the rubber points sticking up all over the insole. No pain, no gain. Walk on, O Seeker, walk on!

Speaking of pain, a few entrepreneurs have profited from Westerners who found themselves unable to sit comfortably in meditation. Most of us don't seem to be genetically programmed to grow legs that move easily into the preferred Asian meditation posture—the cross-legged, pretzel-like twist known as the lotus position. Some Eastern yogis say the lotus posture encloses the body's energy in a special way that enhances meditation. For this reason, and also because it looks stylish and cool, many Westerners have gone through agonizing efforts to remain seated on the floor in some facsimile of the lotus pose while meditating. Thankfully, the New Age marketplace came to our aid with benches, backrests, bolsters, knee pillows, straps, and even elaborate balloon-like chairs—all designed to keep us from suffering while we contemplate the Buddha's First Noble Truth of suffering.

Many New Age seekers became fascinated with pyramids. I remember visiting a famous California retreat center in the mid-seventies and seeing a group of people walking around completely naked except for little pyramid-shaped, copper hats on their heads. They claimed to be experiencing "pyramid power."

Maybe the reason I'm not yet enlightened is because I never hit the right combination of workshops or products. Reading through New Age magazines and their successors, I see that I could still have my biorhythms read, buy a biofeedback machine to monitor my alpha waves, an isolation tank to create a perfect environment for meditation, some full-spectrum lighting to enhance my "light-chemical mood balance," or the Natural Rhythm Futon, which is not, as the name seems to imply, a birth control bed but a way to achieve some kind of moving bodily harmony with one's mattress while sleeping. I could also try the Dream Pillow, which is stuffed with hops. The people who sell dream pillows cite "herbal literature documents" to conclude that hops—not in your brew, but under your head—can promote restful sleep and pleasant colorful dreams.

Over the years I have seen a few poetic come-ons that maybe I should have pursued, like the one that read, "Getting rid of what you haven't got! A one-dollar book on Mantra, Inner Self, Value of Dying, Guru, Flying, Paradise. Enclose one dollar and write to OM"—at an address in California. Another offered a slightly different but equally vague range of eclectic pursuits: "We excel in matters of holistic health, biomagnetism, earth radiation exposures, ESP, the Unexplained. Only $13.50."

.   .   .

Word must have traveled through the Asian guru grapevine that the United States was hungry for Eastern mysticism, because by the mid-seventies a veritable gaggle of gurus had descended on California from the Far East. Every week you would see posters advertising the arrival of another Indian swami or Tibetan lama or Korean Zen master. And for every guru there were plenty of "gurupies," refugees from harsh Jehovah and middle-class materialism looking for a kinder, gentler spiritual home. Many were quite willing to hand over their lives to any man in a turban or robe who smiled at them like Daddy never had. Of course we went for it. And why not? Our society seemed a battleground of competition and jealousy; people were starving to hear that they were wonderful, radiant beings of light and that everything is perfect in the cosmic overview. And it is, isn't it?

As special features producer at KSAN, I was able to interview many of the teachers and gurus who came to town. During an on-air interview with Swami Muktananda, he bopped me on the head with a peacock feather as a blessing, supposedly transferring his *shaktipat* (divine energy) directly into me. I actually went blank for a minute or so, which meant that the listeners heard only silence, and my producer became very agitated about the radio sin known as "dead air." When I came around, I asked Muktananda to perform a miracle that everyone could experience. He replied, "Just feel the blood circulating through your body. That should be miracle enough for anyone."

Tibetan master Chögyam Trungpa Rinpoche stayed totally lucid while drinking an entire bottle of sake during our hourlong interview. He told me that the Tibetans had allowed their monastic institutions to become corrupted and that the Chinese invasion of Tibet was a kind of collective karma. A renegade and "crazy wisdom" master, Trungpa founded the Naropa Institute in Boulder, Colorado, which eventually attracted a huge following of artists and intellectuals, including Allen Ginsberg and Philip Glass.

I also began following the careers of some enterprising Westerners who decided that they were spiritual masters. Many of these self-proclaimed teachers mixed together a few nuggets of Eastern wisdom, a little psychodrama or gestalt therapy, some techniques from the Catholic confessional, and a dollop of Jewish chutzpah or Irish blarney and created their own unique paths to enlightenment. Some of them had real wisdom to offer, but there were several very suspicious characters, to say the least.

In 1976 I interviewed a Dr. Frederick Lenz, who was the director of Eastern studies at the New School for Social Research in New York and who had written a book titled *Lifetimes: True Accounts of Reincarnation.* The book was a fascinating work of sociology, containing well-documented stories of people who recalled their past lives, and I found Dr. Lenz to be a lively talk show guest.

I did not hear of Dr. Lenz again until sometime in 1982, when I picked up a New Age magazine and saw his picture featured in an advertisement. Dr. Lenz was now calling himself "Atmananda" and was promoting himself as some kind of guru. I smiled to myself and tried to imagine his career switch from university professor to cosmic wisdom master. Then, around 1983, I began to see full-page color advertisements featuring a much bigger photo of Dr. Lenz, who had since let his curly hair grow out and was now wearing an Indian-style collarless shirt. The picture was taken with backlight to give his face a glowing halo effect, and he seemed to be gazing out at the world with love.

Dr. Lenz had changed his name again and was now calling himself "Rama, the last incarnation of Vishnu."

That's a pretty heavy claim to make, considering that Vishnu is one of the three principle Hindu deities, the one in charge of preserving the world. The Buddha himself is considered one of Vishnu's incarnations. Meanwhile, the text of the advertisement revealed one of the most audacious self-promotions in this or any other new age. In this ad, Dr. Frederick Lenz, aka Atmananda, aka Rama, listed his past-life resume, an irrefutable list of spiritual credentials:

1531-1575	Zen Master, Kyoto, Japan
1602-1671	Head of Zen Order, Kyoto, Japan
1725-1804	Master of Monastery, Tibet
1834-1905	Jnana Yoga Master, India
1912-1945	Tibetan Lama, Head of Monastic Order, Tibet
1950-	Self-Realized Spiritual Teacher

Rama (Dr. Lenz) attracted a good number of disciples and eventually counseled them all to acquire computer skills, although it is questionable whether those can be taken with you into your next life.

> "We seem to believe we can be reborn without ever dying. Such is the spiritual version of the American Dream."
> —ROLLO MAY, The Cry for Myth

My desire for some great revelation that would awaken humanity or transform the world has led me into some questionable New Age enthusiasms. For instance, in the spring of 1973, astronomers sighted a comet they named Kohoutek and predicted "a momentous astronomical event" when the comet passed near the Earth. New Age seekers adopted Kohoutek as their own, holding rituals to welcome it as a harbinger of the Age of Aquarius. I helped pump up the excitement on my radio broadcasts, but Kohoutek fizzled out. It was barely visible, even to astronomers.

In 1976, the stars of the New Age tried to create cosmic consciousness through satellite television, with a broadcast immodestly titled "The World Symposium on Humanity." Promoted like an entertainment spectacular, the world symposium was held simultaneously in Toronto, London, and Los Angeles and featured Buckminster Fuller, Ralph Nader, Marshall McLuhan, Ram Dass, Dick Gregory, Joseph Campbell, Carl Rogers, Laura Huxley, and Fritjof Capra. I tried to get my radio station to let me cover the event, but the management concluded that there just wasn't enough rock and roll in the program.

New Agers gathered again in 1986, this time for a planetary happening called the Harmonic Convergence, timed to coincide with an ancient Mayan prophecy. I tried to negotiate with the program director of my radio station for time to discuss the event on the air, but he would only let me lead a chanting of "om" for thirty seconds.

It is impossible to gauge the impact of the Harmonic Convergence, but it seems as though the problems of the planet have been growing worse ever since the event. Of course, we can't know why history unfolds as it does, and perhaps the convergence did add some necessary grace note to the music of the spheres. Maybe it was just a little off-key.

. . .

In the late 1970s and early 1980s, I began noticing that the most popular teachers on the New Age circuit were ethereal beings. These disembodied entities were channeled to New Age audiences by people who claimed to be mediums. All at once, it seemed, a multitude of spirit entities had decided to make themselves accessible. Some came from the traditional heavens, many from Atlantis, some from inside the Earth itself—and all of them seemed to have important things to say to the people of our planet at this moment in history. If I may be so bold as to summarize, most spirit guides say something like, "The golden age is coming, and everything is going to be all right, and you are all wonderful beings, and eternal as well. So love each other and be happy." Not a bad message at all.

Seekers may have been drawn to spirit guides after so many of the gurus with bodies turned out to be charlatans. Of course, you still have to go through a medium and risk interference. As Marshall McLuhan said, "The medium is the message."

I attended a few Bay Area psychic fairs to see if I could get acquainted with some of these entities. At one such gathering I found a series of perhaps thirty booths set up around a large conference room. Each booth featured a single female medium (not one male) seated at a table with some amulet before her—a crystal, a feather, a burning candle, or some incense. Some of these mediums looked to me like former fortune-tellers who had once worked the carnival midways but who had discovered that the real money was now in the New Age venues. Several other women in the room had a sweet, spacey, love-the-world vibe, like Deadheads who had taken their acid visions seriously. A few seemed to be former suburban housewives who had been visited by the spirit of Mr. Clean once too often and now wanted to be in a trance that was completely different from housework.

I talked to one of the mediums, a buxom woman with thick lipstick and a pile of permed curls, who said she was channeling a "healing guide named Master Kirk," who would simply come down and put his hands on her shoulders and direct her healing sessions. Another woman told me she was channeling the "White Brotherhood," which was the collective energy of master teachers, including Christ, Muhammad, Buddha, Zoroaster, and so forth. A few mediums were channeling women spirits, and one in particular said she could transfer the energy of Joan of Arc to any female who came to see her regularly.

One thing that interests me is that mediums don't have to take direct responsibility for their predictions or healing; they can always blame the spirits. More than once I have been told by a psychic or medium that they were "having trouble getting through" or that there was some "interference" or that their spirit guide did not feel like talking today. Of course, the spirits may have just decided not to pick up when they heard that I was calling.

For a while, the most famous medium was J. Z. Knight, a Tacoma, Washington, housewife who went to beauty school and then to business college and finally was called to her true purpose in life. One day, Knight claims, she was just standing in her kitchen when an apparition named Ramtha suddenly appeared, saying he was a thirty-five-thousand-year-old warrior from the lost continent of Atlantis. Ramtha also told J. Z. Knight that she was his daughter, and soon thereafter she began channeling her alleged father in a gravelly voice, which eventually attracted the likes of Shirley MacLaine and Linda Evans. Those who believed would call each other "Ramsters" and pay up to a thousand dollars to be in an audience where Ramtha spoke. I tried to interview Knight several times, but I was always put off by her secretary, the medium's medium.

Another former housewife achieved notoriety in a different spiritual circle after she attracted Ram Dass as her disciple. Joya (Green) Santanya, a Jewish Brooklyn housewife in her late thirties with three kids, one day got into her bathtub and started doing breathing exercises in order to lose weight. She reports that suddenly she went into a trance and was visited by none other than Ram Dass's guru, Neem Karoli Maharaj-ji (deceased by that time), who sat down right next to the tub and began talking. The story delighted the spiritual underground as one of those cosmic/comic twists of fate. Everybody's Jewish uncle, Ram Dass, would of course find his new guru in the form of a Jewish housewife from Brooklyn! It was perfect.

The channeling craze spread to even the most respectable New Age venues. At Esalen Institute in 1979, a woman on staff named Jenny O'Connor began to channel "the Nine," whom she described as a group of eight-million-year-old mass-energy entities from the star Sirius. At one point the Esalen staff were consulting with the Nine for advice on how to run the institute.

.   .   .

During a New Age, everybody gets to fashion his or her own religion, mixing and matching pieces of various traditions. At a Christian rally I interviewed a woman who was wearing a jacket with a slogan embroidered on the back that read "Shiksas for Jews for Jesus." When I asked her how she came up with that designation, she explained, "Well, it's true. I am a shiksa, and I'm also a member of Jews for Jesus. So I'm a *shiksa* for Jews for Jesus. It's that simple."

During my own meanderings through New Age workshops I have often felt lost, disconnected from the beliefs and stories that I grew up with and unable to fully adopt those from other cultures that I found fascinating or instructive. Sometimes I would be at a ritual and catch myself thinking, "How odd it is that I am here": at a sweat lodge chanting an old Native American song

or going up to an altar to have my head patted by some
Tibetan lama in a blessing guaranteed to shorten the
number of rebirths I will have. Suddenly I would find
myself asking, "What in the Judeo-Christian heaven's
name am I doing here?" Although I was drawn to rituals
that seemed exotic and mysterious to me, my skeptical
mind would often keep me from entering the spirit of
the event.

Through it all, I always still considered myself Jewish.
Maybe that's because you can't convert out of being
Jewish, just as you can't convert out of being Italian.

In my early travels through Asia, I noticed that a dis-
proportionate percentage of the Westerners studying
Buddhist meditation were Jewish. A few years later, one
of the first large Buddhist meditation centers in America
was founded by four teachers—Goldstein, Kornfield,
Salzberg, and Schwartz. They sounded to me more like
a law firm than a Buddhist teaching collective.

In the meditation community, wide speculation
began as to why so many Jews were drawn to Buddhism.
Perhaps it is because they are such opposites: the stereo-
typical Buddhist is detached, silent, and serene, while
the Jew is sentimental, verbal, and worldly. I sense that
part of the attraction of Buddhism for me was that it
represented an alternative to my own people's intensely
dramatic, emotional approach to life, which often made
me uncomfortable when it appeared in my family or
myself. I was lured by a philosophy and spiritual attitude that did not place such a heavy weight on events
and relationships and seemed more comfortable with

human fate. Over the years I have come to believe that the Jewish and Buddhist cultures are a perfect complement to each other and that their convergence might even produce a wondrous new spiritual hybrid—another kind of middle path.

. . .

Although the New Age contains its share of strange bedfellows, along with many charlatans and snake-oil salesmen, I sense that the movement was and remains essentially a sign of health in our civilization. For some time, many people have found they no longer feel a resonance with the Jewish and Christian tribal stories and myths, and the institutions that house them can seem stodgy, patriarchal, and inimical to contemporary values. The New Age movement still offers alternative expressions of the perennial human desire for connection with the forces of nature and the greater mysteries. It represents the modern search for new ways to understand ourselves as well as methods to both grieve and celebrate that understanding.

With the waning of our inherited religious affiliations, many of us also lost our communities, and New Age events can offer people at least a temporary community of shared belief as well as rituals that unite them. As mythologist Michael Meade says, "Community is sitting together around the same mystery."

. . .

In my New Age explorations, I noticed that the sons and daughters of the white middle classes were the ones most eager for new spiritual experiences. An obvious reason is that we had enough time and money to go on a spiritual quest, and, furthermore, the failure of material affluence, to bring us fulfillment may have motivated our search for the *real* meaning of life. Another reason became clear to me in 1992, when I was asked to teach Buddhist meditation at a gathering of environmental activists.

The retreat was attended by African American Southern Baptists, Latino Catholic farmworkers, Native American tribal leaders, and a group of Caucasian Baby Boomers with their grab bag of Asian and New Age practices, all linked by their involvement in various environmental campaigns. The organizers of the event wanted people to leave their political work behind for a week and gather to share the spiritual traditions that give them sustenance.

On the first day of the retreat, I was somewhat dismayed when only the Caucasian boomers showed up at my meditation class. I began to understand the reason later that evening when Starhawk, a leader of the neo-pagan Wicca movement from California, was scheduled to lead a moon-worshiping ritual. Outside the dining hall the Southern Baptists were talking together, and I overheard one woman say, "I'm not going out there to howl at the moon!" Needless to say, neither the Catholic farmworkers nor the Native Americans showed up at Starhawk's ceremony either. These people felt no need to seek other ways to connect with the mysteries or their own spirituality. In fact, they found some of our New Age practices rather bizarre and in some cases even blasphemous. The white, middle-class boomers, in contrast, were not grounded in any tradition and therefore were open to everything. We joined in the Native American blessings, nodded in agreement with the fiery words of the Baptist preacher talking about Jesus-as-revolutionary, and then went to sit in our adopted form of silent meditation, closing with the traditional Buddhist blessing, "May all beings be liberated."

11

SCIENTIFIC MYSTICS

"The physics of one era is the metaphysics of the next."

—MAX BORN, NOBEL PHYSICIST

EVEN THOUGH MY spiritual path was pointed eastward, it was lined with the signposts of my own culture, especially those announcing the truths of modern science. For instance, when my meditation teacher told me to focus on the impermanence of all phenomena—an important Buddhist door to wisdom—I immediately began to imagine the whirling of atomic particles. It turns out that I was carrying a picture of the changing, insubstantial nature of reality long before I met the Buddha.

Recent generations have been heirs to the great flowering of the scientific revolution that began in the mid-1500s and thoroughly shaped the mythos of our time. We have absorbed pictures of reality painted by quantum physicists and evolutionary biologists, even though we may not fully understand them. My generation was brought up to believe that what the scientists discovered was the truth, and they were basically telling us that we are not who we think we are and that nothing is as it appears.

Throughout my lifetime shocking news has continued to pour out of scientific laboratories and think tanks: The universe is umpteen billion times bigger than previously thought! Matter is made of particles that don't really exist! All of our concepts of past, present, and future are illusions! Human emotions, including love, can be traced to biochemical processes! The human species is a random product of natural selection!

Modem science has in recent decades demanded a new mythology. Not only has it undercut our traditional religious stories, but it's also made us question our place and purpose in the scheme of things. In my lifetime, astronomers have found evidence of at least 100 billion galaxies in the universe, each full of billions of stars, and this number is likely to increase to about 200 billion as telescope technology in space improves. The human- and Earth-centered Judeo-Christian cosmos doesn't accommodate that expanse, yet we can read that the sages of Asia long ago drew a picture of time and space that was even more vast than the one described by today's astrophysicists. In one Buddhist text, for instance, the universe is called three-thousand-fold, because it contains one thousand times one thousand times one thousand world systems similar to our own. Meanwhile, every time the Hindu creator deity Brahma just blinks his eye, another universe is born. Modern physicists now propose a theory of multiple universes, and one wonders if those ancient Buddhist and Hindu sages had an intuitive glimpse of the same cosmic picture.

Today's physics is a primer for mystical visions. Generations born in the mid-twentieth century read in our schoolbooks about relativity, that matter and energy are the same thing, and that time and space are inseparable. In college we might have started hearing about quantum paradoxes, wave-particle dualities, and nonlinear realities, implying that everything in our universe was tightly woven together in a nonmechanical but interdependent way, quite different from what our senses perceived or our civilization had always believed. When we finally began to hear about the Buddhist and Hindu views of reality, there was a deep resonance.

A tenet of Mahayana Buddhist schools is that all material forms are essentially empty, so it turns out that I inadvertently received my first lesson in Buddhism in my high school physics class. The science teacher told us, "Imagine the nucleus of an atom sitting on the floor in front of you. It is so small that if its size is increased millions of times over, it would still only be about as big as a grape, and then the electron going around the nucleus would be the size of a dust mote, and it would be located a half mile away."

My teacher was trying to show us how small atoms are and also the fact that they are mostly (99 percent) made up of empty space. If we look closely enough, we find that the matter of the world is largely lacking in matter. Tiny neutrinos will pass right through miles of dense lead without hitting anything, because even atoms of the heaviest element are mostly empty space.

There are spiritual lessons to be drawn from our understanding of the emptiness of atomic reality. For one thing, we all have a lot less stuff than we thought we had. Furthermore, if our bodies are made of atoms, and atoms are mostly empty space, then what is holding our clothes on? Not only does the emperor have no clothes, the clothes hardly have any emperor! The message is that there is some kind of magic act going on here, and we are all part of a giant illusion. As a Tibetan Buddhist yogi named Tsongkhapa says, "To see truth, contemplate all phenomena as a lie."

A contemporary Zen master used to give his disciples similar advice when he told them to develop a "don't-know" mind. He wanted us to relax our desire to try to understand and predict everything. The physicists certainly helped me develop this "don't-know" mind with their indeterminacy principle, which claims that no matter how hard we try, we can never pin down the physical world. So we can at least relax our minds about that! The scientists also help me with "don't-know" mind because, quite often, I simply can't comprehend what they are saying.

For example, the physicists broke the atom open, again and again, looking for the very essence of matter, and now say they have it down to six quarks: "up," "down," "top," "bottom," "strange," and "charmed," For sure. The top quark was the last to be found, and in the article I read announcing the discovery, the scientists said that this quark has no mass and no dimensions. In other words, it doesn't exist, but they found it anyway. They say the top quark only lasts for a billionth of a second, and therefore only trained scientists with big atom-smashing machines and laser cameras could know it was there, but the scientists themselves have never actually seen one.

I find myself nodding my head in agreement but later realize that the report made no sense to me at all. It seems as though the scientists hold the same position as the ancient shamans, who disappeared into the wilderness for a few weeks or years and then came back to the tribe and said, "Listen up, I just talked to god (or talked to a bush or ate a bush and talked to a rock), and this is what reality is like. Okay?" The modern scientists hold a position somewhat like that, and who else are you going to believe? "Sure, Mr. Scientist, the world is made of quarks that nobody has ever seen."

Hindu and Buddhist spiritual teachers will often try to thwart the rational mind, encouraging us to question our ordinary perceptions and beliefs, and modern physicists have certainly been their allies in this project. For instance, consider the discovery of antimatter. We are told by the scientist shamans that when a particle of matter meets a particle of antimatter, they will annihilate each other. Apparently the big bang created a tiny bit more matter than antimatter, so we got ourselves a universe. But the discovery of antimatter raises some new metaphysical questions for our time: Now we have to ask not only "What's the matter?" but also "What's the antimatter?" and "What does the antimatter have against the matter?" and, more important, "Does it matter?"

The existence of antimatter could mean that the Creator (assuming there was one) was ambivalent about creating the world in the first place. "Should I or shouldn't I?" the Creator asks, as another particle of matter and another of antimatter fall from his/her hands.

Meanwhile, Buddhist and Hindu sages have claimed for centuries that consciousness is the magic ingredient in all creation, the substratum of all appearances. As a Tibetan Buddhist text states, "All things are the illusory, magical display of mind." Through very different methods of investigation, the quantum physicists arrived at a similar conclusion. They say that we participate in the creation of reality by simply observing it. When we aren't looking, there are just waves of energy—"probability waves"—and only when we try to measure or pin the process down does the world of particles and things make an appearance. The Copenhagen interpretation first posed by Niels Bohr in 1920 says, "There is no reality in the absence of observation." Wait a minute! Does that mean if we all shut our eyes simultaneously, reality will disappear?

In answer to that question, there is a story in Buddhist circles about a group of monks who are sitting in a cave in the Himalayas somewhere, holding reality together by paying attention to it. They know that we all have to work out our karma on this earthly plane, so they are making sure that this earthly plane remains intact. You can now relax your mind about reality.

The Buddha was a great scientist, a forerunner of Darwin, Freud, and Einstein, but he taught that certain things were *imponderable.* He said that we could never figure out the first cause, the origin of everything, nor could we unravel all the threads of cause and effect that lead to any given occurrence. Meanwhile, the physicists are still looking for the *theory of everything,* the one summary statement or equation that will sum up everything we know about the physical world. So far, the closest they have come is the *superstring theory,* which says that at the base of all physical reality are these tiny, vibrating strings. (Could this mean that God is a romantic?) The strings are really patterns of energy, vibrating at different frequencies and thereby creating the appearance of different stuff. Maybe the hippies were right when they said, "Just check out the vibes."

Overall, the findings and theories of modern physics lend credibility to the cosmological insight of the Asian sages and helped open the Western mind to Hindu and Buddhist psycho-spiritual practices as well. If the Asian sages had such a good intuitive sense about the vastness of creation and the structure of reality, then perhaps they were correct about nirvana and self-liberation as well. Ironically, Western science became one of our primary gateways to mysticism.

> As I look more deeply, I can see that in a former life I was a cloud. And I was a rock. This is

not poetry: it is science. This is not a question of
belief in reincarnation. This is the history of life
on earth.

    —THICH NHAT HANH, VIETNAMESE ZEN MASTER

I find it fascinating to compare the findings of physicists and astronomers with those of the Asian sages, but the evolutionary sciences had a much more profound impact on my spiritual practice. Evolutionary biologists and psychologists gave me a new way of understanding what I experience in meditation and in my life as well. After all, what we examine in meditation is a living organism, a human being, a body, brain, and nervous system. We may not all be able to be physicists, but to some degree we are all biologists.

If Gautama Buddha were around today, I am certain he would sprinkle his teachings with research findings from the evolutionary sciences. In the Pali canon, the earliest record of the Buddha's teachings, he doesn't talk about gods or cosmic consciousness but instead tells us to investigate our body and emotions, the process of walking, hearing, seeing, and thinking. He says that we should ask ourselves, "This construction (self)—what is its cause, its arising, its ancestry, its origin?" Precisely the subject that the evolutionary sciences are studying.

Recent generations have witnessed a revolution in the biological sciences: revealing what we inherit from other forms of life; giving us detailed descriptions of how our brain functions; showing us genetic links to temperament and personality. The Buddha could use this information to help us see through our individuality and show us how we co-arise and coexist with the world. The evolutionary sciences have become a tool for the spiritual work of self-liberation.

In one discourse the Buddha says, "This body is not mine or anyone else's. It has arisen due to past causes and conditions." It seems that the Buddha intuited some type of evolutionary process that creates our bodies, and now the scientists have filled in some of the details. They say our bodies appear as they do because of the composition of Earth and its changing environments. One example is the fact that only after land emerged did living beings develop legs.

We also know that we co-arise with the sun and the atmosphere and could not live apart from them. The energy that wiggles our fingers and moves our legs comes from the sun. Our bodies are even built out of Earth elements: Our bones are made of calcium phosphate, the literal clay of earth molded into our shape; the liquids in our body have the chemical consistency of the oceans; we literally sweat and cry seawater. This body is not mine. It is Earth's body. It is evolution's body. It's a loaner.

The Buddha understood that if we learn to regard our body as a temporary creation of many different elements and conditions coming together, then we will no longer be so identified with its form or functioning. We will feel more at ease with our physical existence and be more accepting of its inevitable fate.

We regard not only our bodies but also our perceptions, emotions, and thinking as very individual to us, but in fact they are generic. The geneticists tell us that we share nearly 100 percent of our DNA with one another. However, perhaps even more relevant to our identity is the fact that we share over 90 percent of our DNA with mice! We are starting to realize how much of who we are lies in having a standard mammalian body, nervous system, and brain. Our individual personality is just a thin layer of paint over the top of that essential structure.

Although the romantic in me sometimes rebels at this scientific information, I found that I could experience the truth of it in meditation and sensed that this truth could help set me free. What I was learning from the evolutionary scientists began to filter into my meditations and brought me a new sense of myself. I was attaining, not the legendary cosmic consciousness, but rather a biological consciousness. I started to realize that everything I experience in life is based on my being a member of this particular species at a certain moment in biological history. What lies at the bottom of all my personal conditioning is the human condition. The relief that comes from spiritual practice is often due to a shift of identity, but I had always thought that would involve some kind of transcendence. Instead I was shifted into awareness of myself as part of life on Earth.

Evolutionary science also addresses the nature of desire, which is a central focus of the Buddha's teaching. As I watch my mind in meditation, I often see a constant flow of desires: to have, to know, to accomplish, to be secure, to be loved. In the early days of my practice, I would become very frustrated because I could not seem to control or ignore this flow. Then I read an article in *Science* magazine explaining experiments on the lateral hypothalamus of the brain. According to neuroscientist Melvin Konner, our brain is built to function so that "our internal state will be a vague mixture of anxiety and desire—best described by the phrase 'I want,' spoken with or without an object for the verb."

In other words, the flow of desires is not mine. It is organic, generic to my species. We are built to want—whatever. This certainly helps explain our consumer society and why, with all that we have, we remain dissatisfied. But after reading about the organic nature of desire, I became aware of a change in my meditation practice. My own desires began to appear as relatively impersonal and therefore no longer had such a strong hold over me. I didn't have to get caught up in every fantasy or passing whim. I felt as though I was gaining a new freedom from my own biological programming. The desires continued to come, but I could let them flow and let them go.

Another piece of science information that I found useful in my spiritual practice came from neuroscientist Paul MacLean, who found that human beings don't have "a" brain. After years of research at the National Institute of Mental Health's Laboratory of Brain Evolution and Behavior, MacLean announced that we actually have three brains: a reptilian brain, a mammalian brain, and the neocortex or primate brain. These three brains appear sequentially in evolution and also in each of us as we develop in our mother's womb. However, what

MacLean and other neuroscientists have come to realize is that each succeeding brain does not override the previous brain, and, in fact, the reptilian and mammalian brains often seem to control our reactions to the world. Some witty scientists even speculate that the primary work of our new human brain is just to make excuses and rationalizations for the behavior motivated by the two "lower" brains.

In short, each of us has a little lizard and lemur inside of us, and, after learning that, I began to recognize these creatures in myself. For a while I even gave them names: Izzy the Lizard and Larry the Lemur. I found that as I became familiar with Izzy and Larry, I also started to become more comfortable with myself. For one thing, I let Izzy and Larry take the rap for the stream of desires in my mind. *Their* brains are behind it all! When I got to know them better, I even became friends with my little lizard and lemur. I realized that they are carrying the primal instincts for me, especially the survival one, and are therefore looking out for my welfare! I would calm them down at my own risk. MacLean later realized drawbacks to this model, but as neuroendocrinologist Robert Sapolsky wrote in 2017, the triune model is still "a good organizing metaphor" for understanding the brain.

The Buddha understood the power of instincts, long before Freud or the evolutionary biologists. He called them "underlying tendencies," and a lot of his teaching is about how we can train our minds to be more at ease with them and also gain some freedom from their dictates. I found that using facts and metaphors from evolutionary science was helpful to me in this training, and I get similar reports from people who have studied meditation with me.

The evolutionary metaphors also seem to aid in arousing compassion and acceptance for others. In Buddhist teaching, the development of the mind-states of compassion (*karuna*) and loving-kindness (*metta*) are not moral commandments but rather an organic out-growth of seeing who we are. As we recognize our own evolutionary condition, we seem to feel increasing kin-ship with all forms of life and especially with all other humans. We realize that underneath our thin layers of personality we are all joined together at the amygdala, neocortex, thumb, and the upright, forward-facing hip. We are all part of the same project, whether it be sim-ple survival, as some scientists insist, or some unknown purpose designed by a mysterious guiding intelligence. In either case, all humans carry the same legacy of scars and triumphs, the same dreams and limitations, the same experiment in living. We have come together in what paleontologists call the Holocene. We are *epoch* mates, all sharing the same 'cene!

I became convinced that evolutionary science was a powerful tool in the spiritual work of self-liberation, and eventually I wrote a book about it called *Being Nature.* It proposes that in meditation we can actively cultivate a sense of our co-emergence with the elements and atmosphere, cellular life and sunlight, plants and animals, sentience—the whole evolutionary shebang. I have found that a deep calm and clarity and a sense of belonging can arise when people experience themselves in this way—as perfectly natural.

This shift of identity is a vital part of the solution to our current ecological crises. What we need is not a new Bible or new gods or new visions of heaven but rather "a new feeling of what it is to be 'I.'" We need to cultivate the feeling of being at home, of being Earthlings.

. . .

I don't want to sound too messianic about the possibility of shifting identity or even maintaining relative ease or freedom of mind. After fifty years of meditation practice, I still mostly feel like a novice. I have come to realize how difficult it is to achieve any independence from Izzy or Larry or my personality. I don't walk around with a constant awareness of my species self, and I continue to get caught up in desires and identified with my personal drama. But at least now I can blame it all on evolution.

I also try to remember that Rome wasn't built in a day, and *Homo sapiens* wasn't built in even a thousand millennia. The habits of the mammalian heart are well-worn and the neuronal patterns in the brain are tightly wired: the stimulus responses run deep.

However, I believe that meditation has changed my attitude toward the world. I feel that it has made me more forgiving of myself and others and more accepting of life's difficult conditions. What has been most unexpected is that after years of witnessing the workings of my own body and mind, I have grown to be in awe of our human complexity and in particular of our consciousness, the ability to be aware of ourselves. So, while I no longer take my life quite so personally, I have also grown to love it better.

But I have to keep meditating, or else the old habits quickly regain their hold over me and the cynicism returns. That's why meditation is called a practice. If I'm going to cultivate peace and freedom of mind, I have to *practice*. If I want to remember my connection with nature or the cosmos, I have to somehow touch those truths regularly, preferably every day. I have to put on the wider perspectives, like a new pair of glasses, and wear them until I become accustomed to seeing in a different way.

While physics and biology have helped me unravel the spiritual question "Who am I?" the new scientific understanding is not enough. The insights gained by reading science stories are informative but not necessarily transformative. Unless the insights are gradually deepened and integrated into our way of seeing and sensing ourselves, they will remain abstract knowledge—a bunch of facts without any power to change us or relieve our suffering. Modern science has shown us that we live in a much bigger universe than we previously thought, and it has revealed how we have emerged from the natural processes of life on Earth. Now we need to teach our egos their newly discovered place in the scheme of things. The scientific revolution can now be placed in the service of the spiritual.

12

GREEN CONSCIOUSNESS

MOST OF US have lived all our lives with a specter of doom—from thermonuclear war, global warming, and other human-made disasters. These ongoing threats have surely fueled the search for spiritual refuge as well as the call for a new consciousness, one that includes all of humanity and nature in its identity and concern.

The environmental and spiritual movements are twins, joined at the hip, progeny of the late-twentieth-century countercultures, both growing out of the need for a new worldview and way of life. The two movements were fed from common sources: the image of the Earth from outer space, a fragile, blue-green sphere floating in the void; and the understanding that human activity is threatening the biological integrity of the planet, polluting its atmosphere and waters, destroying its forests, and killing off other species of life at an alarming rate.

The environmental cause was a perfect successor for the New Age and hippie tribes: It is about being in harmony with the Tao, adopting the simple-living, non-harming ways of the Buddhists, and realizing the wisdom of indigenous peoples' reverence for the natural world.

There was a good deal of naïve romanticism in the early days of the modern environmental movement, some of it fostered by drug-induced hippie visions of Eden. Many will remember silly posters and paintings of beautiful natural settings, full of waterfalls and tropical trees, with smiling, goofy-looking wild animals walking around and a bunch of naked hippie types frolicking in the midst of it all.

I first heard the world *ecology* from Keith Lampe, a hippie activist who in the late sixties began publishing a newsletter called *Earth Read Out.* (Lampe later changed his name to Ponderosa Pine and fell in love with a woman who called herself Olive Tree. Honest truth!) One day in the fall of 1969, Lampe called me at KSAN to report that the air in Berkeley had become too polluted for him to do his yogic breathing techniques.

In 1972, fifty years ago, the first United Nations Conference on the Environment was held in Stockholm, and a contingent of young San Francisco activists attended, but only to protest outside the official meetings. They saw the environmental crisis as far more severe and widespread than any government had yet acknowledged. Poet Gary Snyder reported back to me at KSAN from Stockholm, "The officials who have come to this UN Conference on the Environment have not come to save the planet but to argue about how to divide it up.

No one speaks for the actual biological and ethnic zones of the planet and the interrelated needs of all beings. No one except for the Hopi Indian delegation."

Some California activists took a life-sized, gray whale-shaped balloon to the Stockholm conference, trying to gain publicity for a proposed ban on whaling. Whales were the first environmental mascot, followed by the proud bald eagle and the cute baby harp seal, but it was the barnacled blowhard, the biggest creature on the planet, that captured the imagination of the first wave of eco-activists.

In 1976 I flew to Japan to report on a music show called *The Dolphin Project*. The idea was to put on a big rock-and-roll concert and simultaneously educate Japanese kids about the plight of whales and dolphins. Performers included Jackson Browne, Ritchie Havens, Warren Zevon, Odetta, John Sebastian, Wavy Gravy, and many others. The never-say-die hippies believed that rock and roll could help save whales, just as our generation's protests and music may have helped shorten the Vietnam War.

Young Japanese jammed the Tokyo concert hall to hear the music, but they seemed indifferent to the whale exhibits set up on the perimeter of the auditorium. Interviewing people waiting in line for the show, I asked one Japanese kid why he had come. He replied, "To see Mr. John Sebastian sing his song from *Welcome Back, Kotter.*"

"And how do you feel about the whales?" I asked.

"Oh, the whales," he said, smiling enthusiastically. "They are very delicious."

.   .   .

By the late 1970s, the environmental movement had taken on the task of Noah, trying to save all species of life. Those who put the issue in political terms started calling nonhuman species the "fifth world." Some who took part were conservationists who believed that biodiversity is necessary for human survival; others, adherents of deep ecology, were simply struggling for the inalienable right of all species to life, liberty, and the pursuit of each other.

The First Annual All Species Gathering and Celebration was held on the autumnal equinox in 1978, at the San Francisco Civic Center Plaza. The Bay Area pagan environmentalists attended this event dressed as their totem plants and animals, in their finest furs, feathers, scales, bark, and shells, accessorized with horns, tusks, plumes, manes, tails, fins, and leaves. Even dragons and unicorns showed up to warn that mythological beings are endangered by human disregard and forgetfulness.

I came in a wolf mask and told the other species that I was a pack journalist on the prowl for a good story. My favorite interview that day was with a man completely covered in strips of bamboo that tinkled when he walked. He said he represented Bapi Bapi, the ancient

African spirit of bamboo, and that the first music heard on earth was the wind playing across a bamboo forest.

Rituals and ceremonies were held throughout the day, and each species had a chance to speak, bark, sound, cry, growl, chirp, laugh (a hyena was present), or whoop. The whoops came from several whooping cranes who announced that there were only 305 of their kind left in the world and that it was getting harder to find anyone with whom to make whoopee. By 2020, thanks to efforts of environmentalists who bred and reintroduced them into the wild, the whooping crane population grew to about 800.

In 1984 a similar group of species representatives gathered outside the Democratic National Convention in San Francisco. Hardly any of the convention delegates came outside to hear what they had to say, but a lot of press showed up. I remember watching one Canadian TV reporter who had the audacity to walk right into the middle of a ritual to deliver his on-camera wrap-up. Planting himself directly in front of a man dressed as a giant bald eagle who was perched on a soapbox and chanting the names of endangered bird species, this reporter, with a concerned look on his face, intoned into the camera, "Antics like these from the lunatic fringe here in San Francisco just might give the Democrats a bad image in this year's presidential election race."

Behind the anchorman, the bald eagle continued to sing out the names of his feathered friends facing extinction: "Eight species of crane, five species of duck, twelve species of parrot, twenty species of pheasant, three species of doves, three species of hawk, four species of owl, the Canadian goose, the African ostrich, the Chinese egret, the red-cockaded woodpecker—"

> *"It's time to make people more important than owls."*
>
> — GEORGE H.W. BUSH, CAMPAIGN SPEECH,
> SEPTEMBER 1992

The fact is that we are now living through a major turning point in the life of our planet—one of the biggest species die-offs in biological history, referred to as the sixth mass extinction or the Anthropocene Extinction. The last time this much life was dying was 65 million years ago when a comet ended the age of dinosaurs. The main reason seems to be the burgeoning human herds spreading across the planet and consuming everything in its path like a plague of very large locusts.

Reading the Endangered Species List can make you incredulous at the enormity of the devastation. The list could be used as evidence in a future Nuremberg indictment for crimes against nonhumanity. The names of the endangered species read like a who's who of the natural world; all our favorite creatures from the television nature shows are on it—elephants, gorillas, the jaguar, leopard, rhinoceros, and many species of deer, turtle, and monkey. The creatures of our fables and poetry are dying: lions and tigers and bears, whales and wolves, the giant sable antelope, the giant armadillo, the Mongolian beaver, the Mexican bobcat, the American alligator, the Jamaican boa constrictor, and the thin-spined porcupine.

It's a wonder that the bells aren't tolling day and night. The Endangered Species List should be read aloud in churches and schools, updated regularly on the front pages of newspapers. Whenever a species is added to the list, perhaps its picture should appear on milk cartons: "Missing!" How else will we know? And every time a species is officially declared extinct, we should have a worldwide wake, saying goodbye forever, and then put up a monument to this form of life that no longer exists on earth.

.   .   .

The counterculture's arguments with American society had a spiritual core and were essentially about the meaning of life and how in American and the advanced Western nations meaning had come to revolve around material wealth and the gratification of individual desires. The issue came into clear focus in the 1970s over the growing consumption of energy and the crises over fossil fuels and nuclear power.

The energy crisis of the early seventies started when oil-rich nations, mostly around the Arabian peninsula, got together to form OPEC, the Organization of Petroleum Exporting Countries, or as we sometimes called them on KSAN, "the O-peckers." This coalition suddenly decided to tie a knot in their big gas hose to the

West until we cried uncle and forked over more money. This was a serious challenge to our icon, the automobile, the symbol of our freedom. We felt that it was our right to go all the way around the planet just to get enough gas to drive ourselves around the block.

Many people in the nascent environmental movement saw the energy crisis as a positive development, a way to slow down the juggernaut called progress and curtail the pillaging of the natural world. Stewart Brand, the editor of the *Whole Earth Catalog,* told me in a 1973 radio interview, "We're in a race between a biological collapse and an economic collapse. I'm cheering for the economic collapse to come in first."

I agreed that the energy crisis at that time was a somewhat positive development—at least when I wasn't caught in a long line at a gas station. In California we could get gas only on alternate days, determined by whether your car's license plate ended in an odd or even number. Many of us were happy to be able to say, "I'm odd."

My Buddhist training had led me to believe that our civilization's speed was its greatest flaw. In meditation I saw clearly how much harder it is to be aware of what I am doing when moving fast. I remain convinced that the real energy crisis is our hyperactivity and that what we need most is to slow down. The ultimate speed bump is heightened consciousness.

> *"During the Industrial Revolution all but one of the seven deadly sins, sloth, was transformed into*

a positive virtue. Greed, avarice, envy, gluttony, luxury, and pride were the driving forces of the new economy."
　　　—LEWIS MUMFORD, *Transformation of Man*

I can visualize humanity's current energy dilemma being played out in a scene by Charlie Chaplin in his role as Everyman. The scene opens with Charlie in a room, enthusiastically building an engine. He is happy and proud of himself as he dances around his invention, deftly putting the final pieces in place and tightening up the screws. At last, after taking out his handkerchief and, with a flourish, wiping off the last bit of dust, Charlie pushes the button and the engine springs to life. But his elation lasts for only a minute because the machine suddenly begins a jerking motion and starts belching out smoke. The room begins to fill up with clouds of smoke, and the engine starts lurching about on its own. Charlie rushes to the window but discovers that it is stuck; then he rushes to the door, but that won't open either. The scene closes with his forlorn face pressed up against the window, miming a plea for help.

As the French philosopher Diderot once said, "What a fine comedy this world would be if one did not have to play a part in it." Unfortunately, we are not in the audience for this show. We are the clowns, and instead of trying to turn our engines off, we keep building more of them, burning more oil, and creating more and more smoke, even today, half a century after scientists and environmentalists warned us of the irreversible consequences. One could point to human overpopulation as a primary environmental problem, but what about the proliferation of oil-burning vehicles and other sources of carbon emissions?

In 1950 there were 50 million cars and trucks on the planet; today there are 1.5 billion! The human population has nearly tripled since 1950, while the vehicle population has increased by a factor of thirty. And people the world over still want private cars. Are you going to be the one to hop in your Chevy or Honda and go tell them that it's too late, we've already used up most of the resources on the planet? Someone has to tell the oil companies and governments worldwide to cut back on oil production and use. By burning up the remains of previous geologic epochs, including the Jurassic, we may well be replicating the atmospheric conditions that extinguished those particular bursts of life.

No matter what gets said in official circles, most wars and regime changes since the mid-twentieth century have been fought for oil and other resources. We may be told that we're fighting to liberate this or that oppressed people, but if freedom is the guiding light of American and European foreign policy, why don't we save the Tibetans and the Uyghurs from Chinese oppression? In fact, Tibet's most valuable resources are Buddhist practices that calm the mind and open the heart, but our leaders don't regard these jewels to be part of our vital national interests.

.   .   .

In the late 1970s, the struggle against nuclear power became the environmental movement's Vietnam War. After Hiroshima and Nagasaki, the post-World War II generations were extremely sensitive to the threat of nuclear radiation. It was the monster we had come to fear, the deadliest poison ever known, and if we messed with it we, like Prometheus, would have our livers eaten out by birds while we were still alive.

But the scientists and corporate executives had convinced each other, and much of the public as well, that they could contain the toxic waste for hundreds of thousands of years to come. What many of us found most outrageous was the fact that this risk was being taken largely to fuel more mindless consumption.

At the height of the energy crisis of the seventies, on my KSAN radio show, my satirist friend Darryl Henriques offered a rapid-fire ninety-second commercial for, a product that claimed to solve all of America's energy problems:

> Are you worried about the energy crisis? Disgusted with high utility bills? Fed up with being an energy victim? Then take control of your life today and make your home energy self-sufficient with US Atom's Home Nuclear Reactor. Small enough to fit into your abandoned fallout shelter yet powerful enough to power your major home appliances, including your washer, dryer, stove, refrigerator, microwave, waffle iron, toaster, coffeemaker, mixer, blender, food

processor, Crock-Pot, electric wok, electric knife, knife sharpener, can opener, popcorn popper, cheese grater, meat slicer, dishwasher, garbage disposal, trash compactor, electric broom, vacuum cleaner, water heater, hot tub, sauna, electric toothbrush, alarm clock, AM-FM radio, tape deck, turntable, amplifier, color television, VCR, electric lights, and your automatic garage-door opener. Not to mention Dad's electric typewriter, Skilsaw, table saw, chain saw, edge trimmer, and Mom's sewing machine, steam iron, curling iron, air dryer, and vibrator, your son's electric guitar, amp, preamp, eco-plex, and wah-wah pedal, and your daughter's electric disco party dress. Your home nuclear reactor comes fully equipped with a lightweight plastic containment vessel and easy-to-follow emergency instructions in case of a mini-meltdown. If you order today, you'll receive free directions on how to assemble a home-sized atom bomb out of your leftover nuclear wastes, enabling you to become a dominant military power in your very own neighborhood. Join the millions who will soon go nuclear with US Atom's Home Nuclear Reactor. Get 'em while they're hot!

In California, the nuclear power struggle centered on the Diablo Canyon Nuclear Reactor, a name that was a nightmare for Pacific Gas and Electric's public relations department but fit perfectly into the symbolic arsenal of the antinuclear forces. Here was the techno-devil himself, holding the lethal poison inside two gleaming steel futuristic domes in a canyon named Diablo.

During the protests, I interviewed a Native American of the Chumash tribe, whose ancestors had buried their dead on the site where the nuclear power plant had been built. He seemed eager to speak, saying, "These corporate people don't understand that the dead are not powerless. At least the Spanish conquerors heeded our warning and didn't build anything in that canyon. In fact, the Spanish are the ones who named it Diablo. Even they knew enough not to mess around in there." Power company officials did not seem to care that they might be arousing the spirits of the dead, but they were hard-pressed to justify building a nuclear reactor just a few miles from an active earthquake fault. Surely tempting the devil.

The protests at Diablo Canyon were great ritual theater, with tactics borrowed from the anti-Vietnam War movement, now more refined. At one rally, affinity groups from all over the Western states gathered at the plant's main gate, and, after chanting praises to the sun, each group climbed the fence to perform some symbolic action or ceremony before being arrested for trespassing. A group called Sympathy for the Devil performed a scene from *King Lear* before they were handcuffed and led away. One group from Mendocino County, called the White Egrets, leaped the fence to plant California poppy seeds and Monterey pine trees. Wavy Gravy, the omnipresent counterculture clown, brought a group called (and dressed as) the Mutant Sponges.

What took place at Diablo Canyon was as much exorcism as political protest, not unlike the Yippies' attempt to levitate the Pentagon in the sixties. But this time the tactics failed: Diablo Canyon was given an operating license and remains "online" today—on the fault line.

The antinuclear movement's fears were justified in late March of 1979 when a cooling system malfunctioned at Unit 2 of the Three Mile Island nuclear reactor in Pennsylvania, causing a partial core meltdown and the release of some radioactive material into the environment. Pregnant women and children were evacuated from a five-mile radius of the plant, but all other area residents were told by a spokesperson from the Pennsylvania governor's office, "Just stay inside your houses and keep your windows shut." That was excellent advice—but only for those with houses made of lead.

The partial meltdown at Three Mile Island energized the antinuclear movement for a march on Washington, on May 6, 1979, which I covered for KSAN news. Dr. Barry Commoner may have been reaching too hard for history that day when he announced to the crowd, "As of today, the nuclear age has died, and the solar age is born." (Some readers may remember that in the late seventies there was a lot of talk about solar energy, renewable resources, appropriate technology, and lowered expectations, ideas that somehow got lost in the corporate takeover of America since then.)

Comedian-activist Dick Gregory also miscalculated the significance of that day in Washington. A decade earlier, Gregory had vowed not to eat any solid foods until the Vietnam War was over, and now he vowed that he would fast until every nuclear power plant in America was closed down. Gregory told the crowd that day that nuclear radiation was the most dangerous enemy they would ever have to face. He said, "I can see war, I can feel racism, I can feel hunger. But I cannot see radiation, I cannot smell radiation, I cannot feel radiation." He told the protesters to go back to their communities and "make radiation real!" Seemingly in response to that call, Allen Ginsberg wrote a poem that contains echoes of his infamous "Howl," this one titled "Plutonium Ode":

> *O heavy heavy Element awakened I vocalize*
> > *your*
> *consciousness to six worlds*
> *I chant your absolute Vanity. Yeah monster of*
> > *Anger*
> *birthed in fear O most*
> *Ignorant matter ever created unnatural to*
> > *Earth! Delusion*
> *of metal empires!*
> *Destroyer of lying Scientists! Devourer of*
> > *covetous*
> *Generals, Incinerator of Armies and Melter of*
> > *Wars!*
> *The Big Bang, the Buddha, and the Baby Boom*

Judgment of Judgments, Divine Wind over
  vengeful
nations, Molestor of Presidents, Death-Scandal
  of
Capital politics! Ah civilization stupidly
  industrious!
Canker-Hex on multitudes learned or illiterate!
Manufactured Spectre of human reason! 0
  solidified
imago of practitioners in Black Arts
I dare your reality, I challenge your very being! I
publish your cause and effect!

.   .   .

It may not just be coincidence that both the New Age and modern environmental movements have their roots in northern California. While visiting the region in 1911, philosopher George Santayana wrote to a friend, "I am struck here by the deep and almost religious affection which people have for nature.... It is their spontaneous substitute for articulate art and articulate religion."

The region spawned the Sierra Club and later, Friends of the Earth, the Earth Island Institute, and the Rainforest Action Network. Greenpeace and Earth First! recruited many of their eco-warriors from northern California, as former beatniks and hippies *and their children* signed up to save the planet. And while Earth First! sent its troops to chain themselves to the thousand-year-old redwoods and sequoias, and Greenpeace sent boats out to confront whalers and ships transporting nuclear wastes, the eco-philosophers of Northern California were developing eco-theories and writing books about the need for a different human nature.

Theodore Roszak, a Bay Area author who wrote the classic sixties treatise *Where the Wasteland Ends,* helped formulate a discipline called ecopsychology. The premise is that our own health and happiness are closely linked to the health of the natural world and behavior that harms one will harm the other. In his book *The Voice of the Earth,* Roszak wrote: "Both the therapists and the ecologists offer us a common political agenda for the good of the planet, for the good of the person. It is simply stated: Scale down. Slow down. Democratize. Decentralize."

Along with ecopsychology, an interdisciplinary approach called eco-spirituality has been added to the mix. Of course, we also have eco-investing, eco-travel, eco-management, and eco-art. Some of it is just eco-tripping, but at least that is better than ego-tripping. In fact, maybe ego and eco grow in inverse proportion to each other.

By the beginning of the twenty-first century, the environmentalists have more or less merged with the New Age spiritual movement. Reconnecting people with their bodies, meditating to diminish aggression and the consumer addiction, shifting identity to include community and nature, the reviving of pagan rituals—these are increasingly understood as the therapeutic and religious components of environmentalism.

In 1976, I interviewed Gary Snyder on KSAN as he captured the environmental ethos and its vital, spiritual heart:

> What we can only hope for is that the eventual economic collapse does not tear the biology down with it as it goes. We have to help ease people's minds so that they are not so anxious about giving up some of their material wealth. The real danger is that the industrialized societies will consume every last shred of timber, every last scrap of wild meat, every last drop of oil, and leave the planet completely ravaged. The best thing that a person like myself can do is to communicate a joyful vision of the alternative, to help allay the fear and smooth the turning to another direction.

13

THE LAST NEWS SHOW

"What I want to see above all is that this country remains a country where someone can always get rich."

—RONALD REAGAN, 1983

THE NEW AGE and environmental movements were blown away by a conservative storm of the Reagan years. Religious fundamentalism, reactionary politics, and rampant materialism began sweeping across the planet in earnest during the 1980s, producing the likes of Reagan, Margaret Thatcher, Menachem Begin, and the ayatollahs. And it continues. Perhaps the dialectic of history is simply doing its yin-yang balancing act, and the conservative epidemic has been in reaction to the liberal "extremes" since FDR and LBJ. Maybe the fact that my friends and I began studying Buddhism had something to do with creating the religious right and later on, the Republican revolution.

In the 1980s I was fairly discouraged most of the time. Although meditation helped me maintain some balance, I felt a constant tension and gloom over a world that seemed to have gone mad for money and power.

I lost my job at KSAN-FM in 1979 after the station switched formats from rock and roll to what is known as urban country. They sure 'nuff didn't want any unrepentant hippie doing news commentary for their new target audience, which someone described as "white-collar rednecks."

But if urban-country music was a contradiction in terms, so was classic rock, the official format of KFOG-FM, where I began working in 1983. I was hired as news director and morning news commentator opposite a disc jockey who called himself Dung. In spite of his nom de plume, Dung was a sweet man and actually quite shy when he wasn't on the air. However, when the microphone was turned on he would switch into his own Wolf Man Jack-like persona and shout, "O-Day!" and "O-Dow!" to express his enthusiasm for his favorite rock music.

I would get up every morning at 5:00 A.M. and within an hour I'd be wearing my headphones, listening to rock songs interspersed with Dung's wild shouts, monitoring the UPI teletype machines, and writing newscasts. This was not what my Shiva baba in India had in mind when he told me to get up before the sun, and I challenge even the greatest of Zen masters to keep their Buddha nature cool under those conditions.

The difference between KFOG and the old radical KSAN was evident in the stations' promotional slogans. KSAN had ironically called itself "Jive 95," but KFOG seriously promoted itself as the "coolest station in the nation." KFOG's classic rock format was aimed at the aging Baby Boomers and reformed flower children, programming rock-and-roll hits they grew up with from the fifties onward. "Rem-mem-mem, re-mem-me-member." (It's amazing how many moments of my life have turned into song cues.)

Shortly after I started working at KFOG, I got a memo about my newscasts, suggesting that my neopagan, pseudosocialist, boho perspective wasn't exactly what the station management had in mind. The memo epitomizes the changes that had taken place in FM rock radio, and in the national Zeitgeist as well:

Memo to Scoop Nisker, 4/5/83

I think we should watch the tendency to sound too much like we're doing news in 1969. By this, I mean the tendency to inject more politicism than truly exists in today's environment. I'm speaking specifically about some of your comments on El Salvador and Southeast Asia this morning. The people who carved the political woodwork of the era gone by are now driving BMWs and making a shitload of money for some computer-oriented business. And while they maintain a casual interest in past political climates, their heads are fully committed to the '80s and the new awareness that guides their beliefs. It is a high-tech society that we are heading toward, and it is extremely important that we are there to accompany this new psychographic with complementary programming, both musically and informationally.

The Grateful Dead Special we just ran was sponsored by the US Army. Jerry Rubin is a broker on Wall Street, and Jane Fonda is a born-again capitalist. This station's information profile must reflect this, both in style and substance.

Let's spend some time discussing this soon. Aside from this point, the only area where you should try to focus yourself better is on the traffic reports at the bottom of the hour.

. . .

I must say, my program director knew what he was doing. He understood that the audience for rock and roll had grown into mortgages and families. People had less interest in radical politics or mysticism or simply didn't have time for them. His programming philosophy was to give aging boomers the musical hits that recalled their past glories and to keep reminding them of their consummate hipness.

In my new radio job I often found myself trying to ease listeners' fears, perhaps because I was struggling a lot with my own. (We teach what we need to learn.) One tactic I used was to put the daily news in a larger context, a grand perspective. I often made the introduction to my broadcasts into a kind of cosmic disclaimer to the news. For example: "The little blue-green planet spins endlessly on its axis, causing the life forms that live on its surface to become dizzy and bump into each other, creating news. And here is a report on some of the collisions that occurred in the past twenty-four hours."

I also tried to cover the latest scientific theories and findings: news of quarks, parallel universes, and galaxy clusters. Bringing some focus to the impersonal forces of physics and astronomy can, I believe, be a balm of no little measure. At least, working on these stories made me feel better. As I told my journalist friends, "You are what you cover."

. . .

There was plenty of despair in my America, as we watched the Reagan and Bush administrations orchestrate an era of deregulated greed that led to the further corporatization and conglomeration of the economy, the malling of our cities, the destruction of ecosystems, and the further loss of our nation's soul. It was especially sad, and even frightening, to see so many Americans blithely going along with the program. It still is.

There was little enthusiasm for serious protest, but the diehard hippies and radicals continued to express their opposition to the government. To commemorate Reagan's second inauguration, a coalition of Bay Area progressives staged the Berkeley Anti-Reagan Festival, or BARF. One booth at the carnival-like event offered people a chance to "Break Nancy Reagan's China," by throwing baseballs at replicas of her kitchenware. Another booth challenged folks to "Pin the Peacekeeper Missile on the Elephant." In response to the Christian fundamentalism that permeated the Reagan government, a few people walked among the crowds at the BARF festival carrying signs that read, "Anti-God."

One of the slogans of the Vietnam antiwar movement had been "Make love, not war." On the day of Ronald Reagan's second inauguration, after it had become clear that the nation was still in thrall to Mammon, I told my radio audience that the radical slogan for the eighties should be, "Make love, not money." *San Francisco Chronicle* columnist Herb Caen quoted me in the next morning's paper and suggested that I put the slogan on a T-shirt and try to make some profit from it.

After his reelection, Reagan asked for a 22 percent increase in US defense spending, starting a major escalation of the nuclear arms race. Only a few months before the election, unaware that his microphone was turned on, Reagan had joked, "My fellow Americans, I'm pleased to tell you today that we've signed legislation that will outlaw Russia forever. We begin bombing in five minutes." Soon after that gaffe, the Union of Concerned Scientists decided to set the "doomsday clock" forward to three minutes to midnight. In January 2022, it was 100 seconds to midnight. The countdown to Armageddon became the subtext of the Reagan-era credo, "Get it while you can." And the dance continues.

. . .

The spiritual search of recent generations has been fueled by a sense of impending apocalypse—and it all began with the atomic bomb in 1945. Those who have lived in the nuclear age have shuddered from the very fact of its existence. It's at the heart of our cynicism and disgust with governments and certainly contributed to our yearning for transcendence. Back in 1962, the Port Huron Statement, establishing the Students for a Democratic Society, made this pronouncement: "Our work is guided by the sense that we may be the last generation in the experiment with living."

The Baby Boom literally got started with the atomic bomb when the two that were dropped on Japan brought an end to World War II. After that, the boomers and the bomb grew up together. The bomb that was dropped on Hiroshima was code-named Little Boy, perhaps because the scientists and generals knew that it was an adolescent and would grow up into Big Daddy nuclear bombs, many thousands of them, each thousands of times more powerful than that "little boy."

At one point there were enough of these man-made monsters to blow up the world at least ten times over, a capacity known as "overkill." I don't remember anybody ever asking why you would want to kill someone more than once. Maybe the generals believed that we could be *dead*-again Christians or dead-again Communists. The only possible consolation is that the second time they kill you it probably won't hurt as much because you'll already be dead.

We boomers grew up ducking under our school desks, as if we could hide from radiation. Many of us came of age with the Cuban missile crisis and grew into maturity with the menace of ABMs and ICBMs and the MX missiles. We lived through the SALT talks and the START talks, during which the United States and Soviet Union agreed to dismantle outdated nuclear weapons and at the same time gave each other permission to build bigger and better ones. The whole mess finally seemed to arrive at its dotage with the Reagan Star Wars plan of the late 1980s. By that time, however, there were so many missiles and antimissile missiles and anti-antimissile missiles, it was hard to imagine how each missile would know which missile to give its dismissal to—unless each missile had a distinct missile whistle, too.

In the beginning, the nuclear arms race was based on the balance of power, or balance of terror, concept, which reasoned that if both sides are capable of destroying the other then neither side will actually try it, a strategy that was officially known as Mutual Assured Destruction, or MAD. Seriously. Did we need any other reason to reject our civilization's wisdom?

During the MAD phase of the nuclear arms race, the Pentagon was even considering plans to install nuclear weapons on the moon. One general explained that if we had nuclear weapons on the moon, then the Soviets would have to launch a strike against our moon missiles at least two days before they could attack the continental United States or else we would be able to retaliate from the moon and destroy them as well.

Another MAD scheme, which apparently received some serious attention in the Pentagon, was to install hundreds of Atlas booster rockets on farmland in North Dakota. The idea was that if the Soviets launched a first strike, we would fire off all the Atlas rockets at the same time, and the combined thrust would actually shift the Earth's rotation, causing all the Soviet missiles to miss their intended targets. Yes, *shift the Earth's rotation!* I don't know if a code name was given to this Pentagon proposal, but I think it should have been called "the Orbituary."

The politicians and generals were even prepared to destroy part of the Earth's atmosphere to make the world safe for their respective ideologies or investments. Until the technology was outlawed by a United Nations treaty on biological and environmental warfare, both the United States and the Soviet Union were designing laser weapons that could burn holes in the ozone layer right over enemy territory. They were planning to target the sun's ultraviolet radiation on crops or military installations or maybe even an entire country. Hell, fry 'em to a crisp if you have to!

The peace movement that remained after Vietnam haI turned its focus on nuclear weapons proliferation and in the late seventies came up with a great hook, called the nuclear weapons freeze. The idea gained so much popularity that even the politicians had to pay attention, and finally, on May 4, 1983, the US House of Representatives voted in favor of a nuclear weapons freeze. Just three weeks later, however, the very same members of Congress voted money for basing and flight testing of the MX missile, a weapon that could not be defended against and one that would surely start another round of nuclear weapons buildup. The freeze melted into mush in the hot air of Washington, DC.

Finally, toward the end of the Cold War, the engineers designed some smaller and "cleaner" nuclear weapons, which the Pentagon felt could be used on selective targets without triggering a full-scale nuclear war. This led the generals to announce a new overall policy called Nuclear Utilization Targeting Strategy, or NUTS. This was either a wild coincidence of acronyms or the most cynical attempt at humor by the generals—admitting that they had gone from MAD to NUTS.

The nuclear arms race spread around the world, and even India, where I first encountered mindfulness practice, developed the bomb (along with six other countries). In order to signal the success of their first A-bomb test to the government officials involved, the Indians used the code phrase: "The Buddha is smiling." The Buddhists cringed.

The nuclear arms race seems to be the most absurd competition ever instigated by human beings, a macho display of almost terminal tumescence. When Little Boy was dropped on Hiroshima, President Truman said, "This is the greatest thing in history." When Albert Einstein heard about Hiroshima he said, "If I had known they were going to do this, I would have become a shoemaker."

The true cost of the nuclear arms race can never be calculated, but that cost includes the fact that the bombs sent a message around the planet that we were a species out of control, crazy enough to destroy ourselves. The anger and despair of all subsequent generations can be traced, in some degree, back to the bomb: it echoes down the years through Bob Dylan's "Talkin' World War III Blues" to the Sex Pistols screaming "No future for you" to Timbuk 3's cynical chorus "The future's so bright, I gotta wear shades." The bomb set off a yearning for spiritual refuge and ignited the call for a new consciousness and way of life.

.   .   .

During their global struggle for power, the United States and the Soviet Union armed the entire world with sophisticated missiles, rockets, jet fighters, bombs, tanks, land mines, and guns, with each superpower selling them to governments and rebel groups, whether or not their leaders were crooks or despots. As long as they said they were against our enemies, they were our friends. In the end, our leaders said that we had won the Cold War, but it seems as likely that everybody lost. War was the only winner.

It is a sad irony that after a half century of preparing for massive conflict between two superpowers, the field of battle suddenly switched to tribal and civil warfare.

The threat of destruction from intercontinental ballistic missiles was replaced by fear of terrorist attacks that could happen anywhere, anytime, conducted by small, secret cadres of dedicated fanatics. The big bombs were no longer of any use, and still the wars continued. And the United States continues to be the major arms supplier to the world. (Still having our "Post-Cold War Clearance Sale!")

One very small sign of hope is that the US Pentagon is now putting some focus on nonlethal weapons, quite a switch from the neutron bomb of the 1970s, which kills people but leaves buildings intact. One segment of the nonlethal arsenal has been "cyber weapons," in which nations attack each other with computer viruses and electromagnetic pulses, trying to destroy the enemy's communication systems, or for use in propaganda dissemination and psychological warfare. During the first Gulf War, the US Army was considering a plan to morph the image of Saddam Hussein onto Iraqi television and show him drinking whiskey and eating pork, both of which are forbidden in Islam. Then, supposedly, the Iraqis would throw him out. That scheme might have worked better than the "smart bombs," which flunked their test. (I think the definition of a smart bomb is one that refuses to go off.)

Another nonlethal weapon in the works is an electronic device that emits low-frequency sound waves that will cause enemy troops to vomit or defecate uncontrollably. What a great idea! We could have wars where nobody gets hurt, just humiliated. "Look, the enemy is pooping in their uniforms!" Yet another of the Pentagon's nonlethal weapons is a chemical that creates such a slippery surface that troops fall down and tanks are unable to maneuver. It's Keystone Cops warfare, and I'm all for it. But the best weapon of all would be a nitrous oxide bomb. As everybody knows, get 'em laughing and they're yours.

.   .   .

Over the years, the counterculture's distrust of the American government had grown into an attitude of perpetual cynicism. After the assassination of John F. Kennedy, many of us began to believe that Washington had been taken over by secret, sinister, forces. Our suspicions grew over time as we saw administration after administration supporting repressive, antidemocratic leaders around the world—Diem, Ky, and Thieu in Vietnam, Marcos in the Philippines, Pinochet in Chile, Somoza in Nicaragua, Arbenz in Guatemala, the shah in Iran, Saddam Hussein in Iraq, "Papa Doc" Duvalier in Haiti, Manuel Noriega in Panama. Our military gave their regimes weapons and instruction, and the CIA trained their secret police and death squads, helping them eliminate their opponents in the name of fighting communism. By the nineties, most of these dictators had fallen, and we received official confirmation of their corruption and usually of some level of US support and complicity.

As the Cold War came undone and national security secrets were declassified, many of our wildest conspiracy theories were proved true. For instance, in the autumn of 1993, newly released documents revealed that in the early sixties the CIA had been in cahoots with the Mafia to assassinate Fidel Castro. Their schemes included exploding cigars, a Paper Mate pen with a poisoned syringe attached, and a plan to spray Castro with an LSD-like substance. The CIA operatives were even experimenting with a chemical that would make Castro's beard fall off. The CIA never did like beards or leftist leaders like Castro.

> *I did not have three thousand pairs of shoes. I had one thousand and sixty.*
>
> —IMELDA MARCOS

In the 1980s, I occasionally called my radio broadcasts *The Last News Show,* reflecting my sense that apocalypse was close at hand. I was not alone in this feeling. The Christian fundamentalists agreed with me, and even members of the government talked about the coming end of days. (Ronald Reagan's secretary of interior, James Watt, told reporters, "I don't know how many more generations we can count on before the Lord returns.") The environmental and New Age movements have been driven by apocalyptic notions, and toward the end of the twentieth century, many people began to sense—at some level of awareness—that we were at a critical moment in human history.

While I don't think we're going to destroy ourselves anytime soon, it sure feels that way sometimes. The litany of ongoing disasters is familiar: endless wars, pandemics, species extinction, global warming, desertification, and toxic pollution. The World Health Organization reported in 2022 that 99 percent of people on Earth do not have consistently healthy air.

As our difficulties multiply, sightings of both Elvis and Jesus are increasing. Religious fundamentalists take to the streets and the airwaves, pointing to the passages in the book of Revelation that confirm our darkest visions. "The apocalypse is here, folks, right on schedule." Scary prophecies about our era can be found in other religious traditions as well. Hopi elders tell us that the time of upheaval is here, and you can read all about it in the Mayan codices. The Hindu scriptures place us in the middle of an age known as the Kali Yuga, a time of decay that is ruled over by Kali Ma, a goddess who is traditionally depicted wearing a necklace of skulls, blood dripping from her fangs. Is it only coincidence that brings these dire warnings from different cultures together? What if some of these predictions are right? Maybe my Buddhist friends and I shouldn't try to "be here now." Maybe we should all be trying to get the hell out of here—now!

It is possible that we are at one of those big moments in history, the dying that must precede the resurrection. In the West, where our own history has become our religion, we give great importance to divisions of time (eras, decades, centuries), and we are just a few years into a new millennium. In the years approaching 1000 CE, there were also dire predictions of the end of days, a response that now seems like nothing but superstition.

There may be no real reason to get so upset. Humans survived the last ice age, Attila the Hun, Richard Nixon, the bubonic plague, thousands of wars, Hitler, volcanoes, tsunamis, hurricanes, and so far, the nuclear arms race. Why should the species fail now, especially when we are so good at toolmaking? Do we face a crisis so different in scope and kind that our past record does not apply? Can we no longer rely on our accumulated skills to figure a way out?

What if we can't? Of course, we're motivated (or forced by instinct) to try to preserve our species. But we're among the most destructive of life forms, and we seem to put ourselves through more unnecessary pains than any other species, as far as we know. Do you think a slug suffers frustration from the slowness of its pace? Does your dog worry about death or whether or not his license should be renewed? Does a bear or a salmon ever yearn for transcendence? Of course other animals feel fear and hunger—the elementary forms of dissatisfaction—but only humans have made desire into a creed. Like a security blanket, we cling tightly to our dissatisfaction. What we have is never enough.

Even though I love my juicer and my flush toilet, I seriously doubt whether humans living in the affluence of America or Europe are that much happier than those who lived in ancient Mesopotamia or in tribes on the great plains of North America thousands of years ago.

They may not have been as physically comfortable as we are, but those cultures had their belief systems intact and felt certain about the meaning of life and death. Besides, in every age happiness is scaled to expectations; life is always a mixture of joys and sorrows, and one god seems to be no better than another when it comes to handing out justice and mercy.

In spite of it all, I can still make a good case for the survival of humanity. Without us, the Earth would lose some of its beauty, simply because there would be no one around to proclaim it beautiful. Let's face it, the other animals are not romantics. If humans were gone, who would adore the seashore or gaze lovingly at the sunsets or groom the horses or hug the dogs or write odes to the lilies? Maybe we should stick around so that the Earth will continue to have a way to love itself.

14

SPIRITUAL POLITICS

FOR MOST OF my adult life, I have felt some tension
between my political impulses and my sense that the
universe is vast and perfect beyond any judgments I may
have or any efforts I might make to change its course. In
1982, I went back to India with the intention of exploring this apparent contradiction. In the midst of all that
cosmic wisdom, maybe there was a secret oral teaching
on social action or a Hindu or Buddhist brand of liberation theology.

On previous trips to Asia, I'd carried a tape recorder
with me but usually set it aside while I tried to erase the
tapes in my head. I once recorded the street sounds of
Kolkata's urban chaos and some wild, devotional chanting in Hindu temples, but on this trip I decided to do
some journalism. I got an assignment to do two documentaries for National Public Radio, one on the legacy
of Mahatma Gandhi and the other on the International
Transpersonal Psychology Conference, which was to be
held that year in Mumbai.

Transpersonal psychology was a relatively new field, put together by some of the more adventuresome psychospiritual explorers in the West, offering a unique approach to life and consciousness. People who call themselves transpersonal practice a kind of experiential, neo-Jungian, Buddhist-flavored shamanism. They investigate non-ordinary states of mind, the psychology of mysticism, and the uses of myth and ritual, all the while inventing new methods of healing and "soul making," as Jung called it. Transpersonal psychologists are trying to revise our definition of who we are and who we might become.

The Transpersonal Psychology Conference at the President Hotel in Mumbai turned out to be a kind of East-West lovefest. All sorts of Hindu swamis and Tibetan lamas came to hear the Western scholars praise and corroborate their ancient traditions, and the Westerners simply begged them to reveal more of it. The twain were finally meeting.

Stanislav Grof, one of the founders of the transpersonal psychology movement, talked about his technique of holotropic breathwork as an avenue to cosmic consciousness; Fritjof Capra described the correlation between science and mysticism; physicist David Bohm offered his theoretical "implicate order" as a new name for the cosmic Oneness; Rabbi Zalman Schacter-Shalomi spoke on his concept of eco-kosher and the Jewish understanding of the absolute. When I interviewed Schacter, he assured me that the Buddha's First Noble Truth of suffering was discovered independently by Jews, expressed primarily through the "oy vey" mantra.

Mother Teresa spoke at the transpersonal conference, and the Dalai Lama was scheduled to appear but fell sick at the last minute. A couple of uninvited barefoot sadhus and swamis tried to crash the event but ended up sitting out on the lawn of the hotel, offering their morsels of wisdom to anybody not satisfied with the cosmic supper being served up inside.

After the transpersonal psychology conference ended, I traveled around India to gather tape for the documentary about Gandhi. A quarter-century after his assassination, all that was left of the Gandhian movement were some scattered ashrams and community centers where a few young social workers experimented with appropriate technologies and cottage industries, while the older veterans of Gandhi's independence campaign sat around and told stories about their exploits and early idealism. The scenes were reminiscent of some I had seen in Berkeley, where aging radicals came together at small protest rallies and talked about the good old days.

My search for Gandhi's legacy took me to Bodhgaya, the village where I had learned how to meditate. During my previous visits, I didn't think much about Gandhi because I was too busy trying not to think. It turned out that right down the street from where I had been meditating was an ashram devoted to carrying on his work, ministering to the poor and promoting the Mahatma's vision for a sane society.

The Gandhi Ashram in Bodhgaya was run by a man named Dwarko, a stocky, intelligent Bengali in his late fifties. He had been working for thirty years in Bihar State, one of the poorest regions in India, and during that time he had supervised the construction of thirteen new villages for peasants who were members of the so-called rat-eaters caste. These people did not even have rice to eat for more than six months out of the year and often were forced to eat leaves and roots, which served as garnish for one of their main sources of protein: rat meat. Almost all of these villagers lived below the Indian poverty line, which is about five dollars a month. "We started from minus zero," Dwarko says of the people he works with, "and we still haven't reached zero." The villages Dwarko helped build for these people were part of Gandhi's plan for India after independence, his so-called constructive program. Like most people, I had been aware of the Mahatma's leadership in the struggle to free India from British rule and his commitment to nonviolence, but I hadn't known about his program for village socialism in India or his critique of capitalism or his ideas about education and ecology. In fact, Gandhi had a comprehensive design for a cooperative society, which is not talked about very much in India, or anywhere else in the world for that matter. Neither communists nor capitalists wanted anything to do with the Mahatma's idea of a decentralized, spiritually based village republic. As Dwarko and other Gandhian workers explained it to me, I was amazed at how similar the Mahatma's ideas were to those of new-paradigm thinkers in the American counterculture. Like Gandhi, they had rejected the twentieth century's idea of progress.

After gaining independence, India's political leaders ignored Gandhi's constructive program. Nehru and his colleagues were infatuated with the West and determined to turn their nation into a modern industrial state. Gandhi had lived in London at the turn of century and saw the slums of Liverpool, and he concluded that industrial capitalism was an evil. He saw that it led to the concentration of wealth and power, the creation of big cities full of displaced people, and a consequent breakdown of ethics, spiritual values, family, and community. Gandhi saw the problem as a matter of size and scale. In a small pamphlet that I picked up at one of his ashrams, I read this quote of his:

> Society based on nonviolence can only consist of groups settled in small units or villages, where voluntary cooperation is the condition of dignified and peaceful existence. This end can only be achieved under decentralization. Centralization cannot be sustained and defended without force. It is not unreasonable to presume from the state of the West that its cities, its monster factories and huge armaments are so intimately interrelated that the one cannot exist without the other. The nearest approach to civilization based upon

nonviolence is the erstwhile village republic of India.[8]

Gandhi was against globalization before the world even realized that it was happening. He was New Age even before there was one. He believed that "small is beautiful" and advocated appropriate technology as an alternative to large-scale industry and mass production. He also believed that all living beings are equally sacred, making him one of the world's first deep ecologists. He called his deep ecology "biological nonviolence."

Gandhi knew that we all will have to sacrifice in order to achieve a new society, and he called on people to live simply. In his own life, Gandhi set standards of simplicity that few people would even attempt to meet. He once visited the king of England wearing only a loincloth, shawl, and sandals. Later, when questioned about the propriety of his attire, Gandhi said, "It was quite all right. The king was wearing enough for both of us."

When he died, Gandhi left only a few personal possessions: a figurine of the see-no-evil, hear-no-evil, speak-no-evil monkeys, his spectacles and walking staff, a few pieces of homespun clothing, and his spinning wheel. As rural and old-fashioned as his vision may appear to those of us immersed in modernity, we may yet find ourselves asking Gandhi s advice for ways to get out of the complicated tangles of our global world.

. . .

The Dalai Lama shares Gandhi's understanding of social problems. By chance, I was staying in Bodhgaya when the Tibetan leader arrived to give Buddhist teachings to his people living in exile in eastern India. I wanted to include the Dalai Lama in my documentary, and since this was before he was awarded the Nobel Peace Prize, I was easily able to arrange a meeting with him.

Awed by the prospect of interviewing "His Holiness," as most Buddhists refer to him, I crafted my questions carefully and in a serious tone began the interview by asking, "What do you think Tibetans have to teach us in the West?" The Dalai Lama thought for a moment, and then, eyes twinkling, replied, "We can teach you how to make Tibetan butter tea." He then burst into laughter.

Later in our talk, the Dalai Lama said that he agreed with Gandhi's ideas and remarked, "My economics is sufficiency." Like Gandhi, the Dalai Lama believes that after basic needs are met, true happiness comes not from material wealth but from the cultivation of peace, both inside and outside. That seems to be the bottom line of spiritual economics and politics.

My last stop in India was at the Gandhi memorial in New Delhi. At the entrance, Gandhi's favorite talisman was carved in stone: "Whenever you are in doubt, or when the self becomes too much with you, try the following expedient. Recall the face of the poorest and the most helpless person whom you have ever seen, and then ask yourself if the next step you contemplate is going to be of any use to him."

When I returned from India, I produced a documentary that drew on parallels between Gandhi's ideas and those of the New Age and environmental movements. The connection had been confirmed for me at a Gandhian ashram in Warda, India, where I found a dog-eared copy of the *Whole Earth Catalog* on the director's desk. In my radio program, however, I tried to downplay the fact that Gandhi's ideas were largely ignored in India. If they didn't play in the Punjab, then how could they play in Peoria? But as Gandhi once said, probably with a twinkle in his eye, "Truth does not become error just because nobody believes it."

It seems clear to me that our current economic and political order will have to change and that any real change will necessarily involve some kind of spiritual transformation. The well-being of all life demands a shift of consciousness from the acquisitive, warlike habits of our species, and that will require some work on ourselves as well as on our governments. Maybe the failure of so many socialist experiments has something to do with the fact that they banned religions, pulling the mystery out of their world, leaving no rituals or other methods to create awe and humility in people or a sense of the divine.

If we intend to change our way of living, we will need a new reason to live, some goal or value beyond private gratification or the accumulation of wealth. We will have to learn to want different things, and this will require a new definition of happiness, a new meaning of life. The religion of consumerism simply cannot feed us all with salvation.

Perhaps what we need more than anything is to learn how to relax. Simply put, that may be what the New Age movement is all about: learning how to relax and just be. It seems that if our survival is truly at stake, the last thing we want to do is relax, but in our case it may be a central part of the solution., We seem driven by anxious urges to hoard and gorge, perhaps appropriate to the well-being of small tribes of hunter-gatherers but now out of date. Our current dilemmas appear to demand a less aggressive response to the world.

That is why meditation is a political act. It's subversive to gain some control over your desires, especially the excessive kind that have been stimulated by all the advertising messages. It's an act of dissent to sit down and do nothing, to be content with this moment, this breath, this mysterious *aliveness*. And when you aren't producing or consuming, then you are sabotaging the system. Meditation can be understood as a sit-down strike.

The current spiritual revival in the West may be motivated in part by a growing realization that our way of life is not sustainable and, furthermore, has not brought us the expected happiness. One consumer survey recently found that the average American in the year 2000 had twice as much material wealth as he or she did in 1950 and, according to studies at the National Institute of Mental Health, was ten times more likely to be diagnosed as clinically depressed. Experts in the fifties said we were headed for a "leisure society" and would soon have the problem of figuring out what to do with all our free time. By 2000, the average American was working five to ten hours a week more than in 1970.

In the 1980s, a few people jumped off the treadmill of consumption and started a neo-Gandhian movement known as "voluntary simplicity." Unfortunately, not enough people volunteered. Maybe a recession or major economic downturn would be good for us. We could just think of it as involuntary simplicity. If our way of life has to change, perhaps the only question that remains is whether it will be voluntary or involuntary.

If history has anything to teach us, it's that our way of life is certain to change. From the promontory of the twenty-first century, we can look back and see that no civilization or empire lasts forever. In 1926, Oswald Spengler pointed this out in *The Decline of the West,* which Joseph Campbell called one of the most important works of the modern era. After a thorough study of history, Spengler found that all civilizations go through a typical life cycle. In the beginning, a fresh culture arises, full of new ideas, artistic forms, and innovative technologies. If enough people adopt the new culture, it turns into a civilization, the way of life for an entire nation or region. Inevitably, the citizens of a successful civilization become convinced that they alone are the holders of truth and must spread their ways to the rest of the world or are simply convinced that they have the right to plunder the world's resources. An empire then emerges, a sign of the final stage of the life cycle; in every historical case, imperialism is the beginning of the end.

Spengler does not assign fault or blame; this is just the way things happen in history. Civilizations are temporary contrivances, as impermanent as their ideologies, fashions, and monuments. Like some wild ecosystem growth, climax, and decay, the life cycle repeats over and over again with only slight variations. The script is so similar that you might imagine each empire passing on to its successor—along with the keys to the colonial treasure—the blueprint and instructions for the rise and fall.

We can see the imperial story repeating itself throughout the ages: in Mesopotamia and Babylonia; in the civilizations of the Mayans, Aztecs, Egyptians, Greeks, and Romans; in the powerful Chinese dynasties and the vast Ottoman Empire. Today these realms are nothing but tourist attractions, ruins for climbing on and picture-taking.

More recently, we had the European empires: the French, Spanish, Portuguese, and British. In the mid-twentieth century the Brits were proud to say, "The sun never sets on the British Empire." All that is left of it today are those few chilly little islands in the North Atlantic, and you could say that the sun hardly ever rises on the British Empire.

The United States took over the European colonies with Coca-Cola, television, and dreams too rich to ever be fulfilled. Although we are too self-righteous to call ourselves an empire, we are surely the mother country of worldwide economic and cultural hegemony.

After the terrorist attacks of September 11, 2001, many Americans began asking, "Why do they hate us?" One simple answer was because we are rich. We live in a castle on a hill, and those arrayed outside the gates have much less than we have and, in many cases, very little at all. Through our own movies and television, distributed worldwide, they are all watching us consume our feast, and furthermore, they see us exercise our freedoms to the point of what is blasphemy to them. Is it any wonder that some people might want to throw rocks at us?

Another reason other people might hate us is the fact that the United States government has been acting more imperial since 9/11, sending troops all over the globe, not so much to spread our democratic ideals as to pillage or protect resources and corporate markets. Our government has been taken over by moneyed interests who are busy making the world safe for profit.

The United States is beginning to exhibit some of the classic signs of decay. In *The Decline and Fall of the Roman Empire,* Edward Gibbon listed as some of the causes of Rome's decline a bloated and overextended military, widespread political corruption and increasing plutocracy, public apathy and cynicism, wild swings in the economy, spectacles that strive ever harder to keep the citizens diverted and entertained, plus the massive influx of colonial peoples and their customs and beliefs into the mother country. Sound familiar?

If decline is to be America's eventual fate, then perhaps we shouldn't fight it. Maybe a better approach would be just to give up now, without a grim, protracted struggle. In the past, citizens of the world's superpowers have stubbornly tried to hold on to their privilege and opulent lifestyles, resulting in prolonged wars and great suffering for many, both at home and in the colonies. If we could only learn from the mistakes of history, we might be able to redraw the blueprint for the decline and fall, setting a new example for all future empires to follow. As the Dao De Jing says, "Yield and overcome."

A vision of what a voluntary American decline might look like came to me in a wild meditation fantasy. At one ten-day meditation retreat, I was feeling bored with my relatively empty mind when a new social philosophy began channeling itself through me, uniting my spiritual and political ideals. It goes by the name of Zen socialism, and it just might be the next step in the dialectic of history. Okay, you laugh. But this time we would stand Karl Marx on his head, and in that yoga posture he might be able to realize the importance of relaxation in the coming revolution. Zen socialism refers to a collective letting go, a voluntary and coordinated surrender of our greed for more power and wealth, a joyous removal of the harness of ever-increasing production and consumption.

Under a Zen socialist government, the United States would simply go to the United Nations and announce to the world that we want to resign as a superpower. We would declare that from now on we want to be just an ordinary nation—a simple people, living in freedom.

What a glorious moment in history it would be! Never before has a great world power let go with such dignity and purpose.

The end of empire may be nothing to fear. Remember that Rome didn't *decline* in a day either. During the decline, a lot of Roman citizens probably didn't even notice it was happening, and a few centuries later they started calling themselves Italians, and they seem to be doing fine today.

If the United States resigned as a superpower, our government could plan some temporary social programs to help ease our transition to ordinary nationhood. I envisioned a five-year plan called "The Great Leap Backward." Guided by this slogan, the government would set up public works projects similar to Roosevelt's New Deal of the 1930s, except these programs would help us wind *down* our economy. This will be the *"New Age New Deal."*

One of our biggest challenges will be to unstress, to slow ourselves down. To effect this change, the government would establish a new agency called the Department of Meditation and Therapy. The DMT would set up deprogramming centers around the country, teaching overachievers and hyperactive workers how to become less productive members of a less productive society. The Department of Meditation and Therapy would pay people by the hour *just to work on themselves.* The entire nation could work with the mantra "Enough! Enough! We've got enough stuff."

Another public works program could be established for those who do building and construction work. *Dis*-assembly lines would be set up, employing people to take apart the cars, melt and separate the steel back into ores, and shovel it all back into the ground. There would be plenty of work breaking up unnecessary freeways and parking lots. Meanwhile, the Army Corps of Engineers could take on the job of digging up the dams they have built and letting the rivers run free again. What a glorious national task it would be! A cry would go up around the country: "Let's make the world safe for nature!"

As we begin to adjust to our intentional decline, the New Age will flourish. Ordinary Americans will begin growing sprouts on their kitchen windowsills; community vegetable gardens will spring up on suburban lawns; and clothes will be hung out to dry from the windows of condominiums. Home remedies, midwives, and composting will become common. There will be two chickens in every garage! What it comes down to is that the Great Leap Backward is exactly what the ecologists and neopagans have been calling for: The New Age is really just planned underdevelopment.

To pay for and administer all these public works projects, the Zen socialist government could simply cut the Pentagon down to size, along with a few of the so-called intelligence agencies. After resigning as a superpower, we certainly wouldn't need three-quarters of a trillion dollars a year for our military. We could cut 90 percent of that budget to pay for universal health care and education, decent mass transit, and environmental cleanup. The other 10 percent of the military budget should be enough to support a small standing army to help out in hurricanes and other natural disasters, with enough funds left over to keep a few nuclear submarines in operation—just in case the Russians or North Koreans get some crazy wild ideas about attacking us.

My meditation fantasy about a Zen socialist government doesn't seem to be the direction the world is headed. In fact, recent history has shaken my faith in the viability of any alternative to greed, hatred, and delusion writ large and even made me question my own beliefs and understanding. Do Buddhist spiritual practices, alternative paradigms, and simpler, eco-sustainable lifestyles have any real future? Is it possible that the information capitalist global economy will course-correct and humanity will come to a new equilibrium? Could this New Age vision be nothing more than nostalgia for a past that never existed and hope for a future that was already impossibly retro forty years ago?

One of my favorite aphorisms is from the Daoist sage Zhuang Zhou (Chuang Tzu), who says, "Those who know they are fools are not the biggest fools." With that as my guiding truth, I won't presume to predict what is going to happen. But I remain convinced that recent countercultural ideas and creations—deep ecology, sustainable living, earth-based rituals, methods of altering consciousness and shifting identity, "Scale down. Slow down. Democratize. Decentralize"—will make more and more sense in the coming years. I have a feeling that we are going to be spending the rest of this century making up for the mistakes of the last few.

> *Tribe follows tribe and nation follows nation*
> *like the waves of the sea.*
> *It is the order of nations, and regret is useless.*
> *Your time of decay may be distant but it will*
> *surely come,*
> *for even the white man, whose God walked and*
> *talked with him as a friend,*
> *cannot be exempt from the common destiny.*
> *We may be brothers after all. We will see.*
>
> — ATTRIBUTED TO CHIEF SEATTLE, 1855

15

COMING DOWN

FOR A TIME we were a movement that believed we would change the world. During the era of the 1960s and seventies, there seemed to be a growing social force consisting mostly of young people filled with revolutionary energy and ideas about transforming consciousness and society. In the years after, that movement lost its hold on most of its followers. Some went off to find nirvana, others joined revolutions for racial and gender equity, gay rights, and reversing climate change, but many if not most dropped back into mainstream America as easily as they'd dropped out.

For many of my friends, the decades following the years of protest and experimentation were a time of compromise, of reconciling ideals with "reality," both personal and political. We learned that it's tough to turn the world around or to quiet our minds and open our hearts, and so we decided to face the consequences of growing up, making a living, raising a family, and now we're grandparents and great-grandparents with enough time to look back at it all and wonder.

Having a spiritual path did not make me immune to the shocks and disappointments of life in the world, and as I grew older I often had doubts about the course I took. I'd wonder, "Maybe I should have lived more like my parents did." As I saw what was going on around me in the silicon and housing bubbles, I'd think, "I forgot to buy a house," and "Darn, I forgot to get rich."

I did remember to have a child, a daughter named Rose. But like so many members of my generation, I didn't have a single nuclear family. Although it would have seemed bizarre to our grandparents or even my parents, almost everyone I know has had at least two marriages, or several live-in lovers, and other shifting and mixing of relationships. We seemed to be a bunch of lost atoms trying to find the right pod of molecules to join, creating a kind of antinuclear family. Freud would have blamed it all on the sexual revolution, which in my mind was one of the most significant of all the social changes that swept through the late twentieth century and whose effects are now so pervasive few can remember life before it happened. A few of us couldn't quite figure out what to do with the sexual revolution, though, except to have sex.

Despite having had a fine marriage and an extended family and friends, I sometimes feel nostalgia for the idealized American family—the picket fence variety that became so hard for many of us to find—longing for the fantasy that was projected in my boyhood in the ads, on the sitcoms, and in the minds of my parents.

Like many, I clashed a lot with my parents in my hippie days, and it wasn't just over the length of my hair. Our views and interests were very different, and I felt somewhat guilty and uncomfortable around them because I had rejected their dreams for me. I had even given up on their God. As Ram Dass was fond of saying, "I'm only Jewish on my parents' side." Sometimes I tried to protect my parents from parts of my life that might have disturbed them. Once, on my way to study Buddhism in India, I told my father that I was going to be taking courses in Asian psychology, which wasn't that far from the truth but did not imply that I was investigating a new religion. I once tried to introduce my parents to meditation, but within minutes of beginning to watch his breath, my father fell asleep and began snoring. My mother immediately burst out laughing and said, "That's what I do every night. Snoring meditation."

. . .

In the years following the protest era, an unusual number of my Berkeley friends who had been hippies and activists went into the food business, strange as that may seem. A few of them started a co-op called the Cheese Board, while others opened restaurants and catering services. Maybe they couldn't stir up a revolution, but they did create California cuisine.

I did my share of selling out and probably would have sold out more if there had been a good offer. For extra money I did radio commercials for tennis shoes, computers, and even cell phones. I needed the money. In the eighties and nineties, many former hippies who had once quoted the *Tao Te Ching* started quoting the Dow Jones averages instead. The Beatles could have sung, "He was a da-aa-ay trader."

Nowhere was the collapse of boomer idealism more evident than in the fortunes of rock and roll itself, as more and more of its stars began leasing their songs to the corporations. The Beatles rented their song "Revolution" to help Nike sell shoes, but that wasn't such a terrible sellout when you consider that the song was actually counterrevolutionary, with the lads singing "Don't you know it's gonna' be ... alright." A bigger sin was Steppenwolf selling "Born to Be Wild" to Ford Motor Company, or the Who selling their road song "Goin' Mobile" to GTE Mobilnet (now Verizon Wireless). Especially confusing was to hear Crosby, Stills, and Nash's song "Teach Your Children Well" in a commercial for Fruit of the Loom. I had no idea that "teaching your children well" had to do with their choice of underwear.

To my mind, the second-worst sellout was when the Youngbloods leased their great anthem, "Get Together," to the Pepsi-Cola Company. How many times, at how many rallies, and for how many causes, did that anthem ring out to raise the common spirit? "Everybody get together try to love one another right now...." Sold to the sugar and caffeine pushers of America!

The unkindest cut of all was Bob Dylan allowing his song "The Times They Are a-Changin'" to be sold to a New York accounting firm. That song was a boomer national anthem, the "Stars and Stripes Forever" of Woodstock Nation, announcing our paradigm shift, our Aquarian takeover. One true believer said that Bob must have sold the song as a way of mocking the system from within, but it's also possible that he was just having a cash-flow problem.

> *"In sacred space people suffer what they need to suffer, and fear to suffer."*
>
> —CARL JUNG

Perhaps it was my sorrow at the waning of the counterculture and its hopes and plans, or maybe just my own midlife crisis, but one day I found that I was in mourning. I discovered this at a gathering of men. Yes, I did some of that, too. My identity as a man was something I had never even considered until the women's movement arrived, along with the coming out of many in the LGBTQ+ community. In an era of identity crises, we eventually got down to basics, and just as in the sixties I had begun to think of myself as part of a generation, in the late eighties I found myself joining a gender. Deconstruction rules.

In 1977 I interviewed Robert Bly for my radio show on KSAN. At the time, Bly was just beginning to focus on men's issues. He was mostly concerned about our inability, as individuals and as a nation, to grieve, or to face what Jung and others called "the shadow." In Bly's opinion, Americans who were turning to Asian mysticism were going in the wrong direction; we did not need to transcend, to go upward, but instead needed to descend, to touch down on earth and go into the grief buried deep in every American psyche. Bly was passionate about it, saying, "When I meet spiritual people in this country, they're just too damn cheerful. The American way is to be cheerful, not to talk about the darkness or the crimes. We have never grieved for the Indians who we slaughtered and whose land we stole, and we have never grieved for the Vietnam War. If the Zen Center in San Francisco would hold a public ceremony to grieve for the Vietnam War, then I could believe that spirituality was taking hold in this country." Thirteen years later, Bly himself organized a public ceremony at Fort Mason in San Francisco, where five thousand people came to smear ashes on their faces and join in a community wailing over the Vietnam War, a conflict that had ended almost two decades earlier.

By that time, Bly was also teaching men's retreats, with a focus on the shadows in the American male psyche. A friend of mine, Buddhist teacher Jack Kornfield, began attending these retreats in the mid-1980s, and one year he convinced me to come along. The retreat took place in a redwood forest camp in Mendocino, California, and was led by Kornfield, psychologist James Hillman, mythologist Michael Meade, and African tribal elder and ritualist Malidoma Somé.

After registration I was asked to choose a clan that I would belong to for the week: Red Deer, Lion, Raven, or Trout. My cynicism flag went up: This sounded too much like Boy Scout camp. I finally decided to become a raven, because they are tricksters in many mythological traditions, and I thought I might be able to enter that familiar outsider's role. However, the ravens at this men's retreat were given a serious agenda, written out for us on our clan assignment sheet:

> The ravens catch the shadows of men and walk among the bones of the battlefields. They never neglect the darkness. Bearing hard, truthful messages from the invisible, they nourish the lonely soul with gifts of intuition, for their intense sharpness sees the jewels others miss.

It was difficult for me to find the raven within, and I kept resisting the activities of my clan. I became acutely aware that I was protecting myself with cynical judgments about the retreat, staying on the fringe. As the week progressed, however, I was drawn into plans for a grieving ritual.

Malidoma Somé organized the event, based on the funeral ceremonies of his West African tribe, the Dagara. Spiritual leader Malidoma is a fully initiated Dagara man, educated in Europe and the United States, whose village elders sent him to the West to teach "village values." After meeting him, Bly and Meade recruited Malidoma to help teach the men's gatherings.

During a discussion one day, Malidoma told us that he had been trained by his tribal elders to see people's spirits, or auras. When he first came to the United States, he said that he was frightened by the sight of so many people "who had a big hole where their necks should be." Their heads did not seem connected to their bodies. Before his second trip to the West, Malidoma asked his elders to remove this power to see people's auras.

As we prepared for the ritual, psychologist James Hillman explained, "Grief in our culture takes the posture of solemnity. People just stand around in the church or at the cemetery, and it's all bowed heads and muffled sobs. Visually, it resembles shame as much as grief." According to Hillman, the grief gets stuck inside. It doesn't move, and it poisons the soul.

The grieving ceremony at the men's retreat took place on a field between two stands of redwoods. At one end of the field was "the village," the gathering spot, where men played drums and sang a sorrowful chant. On the other end of the field was a sanctified area bordered by stones, which represented "the other world." In the Dagara ritual, this was where the dead were laid out, but for our purposes this became an area that contained all our losses—not only the imagined bodies of those close to us who had died, but also the America that had disappointed us, the Vietnam War, our dying cities, the lovers who had left us, the sorrow of all our enormous twentieth-century confusion. We symbolically placed these losses in the sanctified area and then went back to join the drumming and chanting.

The ritual turned out to be African gestalt therapy transplanted in North America. Its intended purpose was to break open our hearts, and for most of us it did. In the West African villages, the mourners try to throw themselves over into the sanctified area, to follow their loved ones into the other world. At the men's gathering, we were told that when we felt some grief arising, we were to walk or dance or even run across the field over to the shrine area. Once there, we were to hurl our grief into the other world.

It's difficult to create a new ritual or to transplant one. It requires an agreement by a community that certain acts and words will have a shared sacred meaning. Without time and tradition to give significance to a ceremony, whether it be celebration or mourning, the effect can feel contrived. So much depends on the participants' ability to release themselves into the event, and that requires a kind of foolish bravery. Sometimes I can let go, and sometimes I can't.

I resisted the grieving ritual successfully for an hour or so, but as I watched other men begin to weep, I started to feel the sadness inside myself. At first I felt a little embarrassed to sob in front of other men, but as I let it happen, my sadness soon changed from something personal into sadness for everybody's sadness. I found myself crying for all six billion of us and for everyone who had ever lived in this fragile, self-conscious human form.

Aside from the catharsis it provided, the grieving ritual made me aware of the fact that I usually keep a certain distance from my emotions. I had been afraid or embarrassed to feel my own sorrow, but in suppressing it I had also cut myself off from a good deal of intimacy with the world. If I close my heart to sorrow, no matter how slightly, it also gets closed in equal measure to the emotions of love and joy. For any taste to exist at all, you must have both the bitter and the sweet.

I realized as well that I often hid inside my meditation practice, using it to maintain my distance, to stay an outsider. Others who I have spoken to agree that the equanimity developed in meditation can sometimes turn into a sterile detachment. Instead of feeling more human after cracking open the shell of ego, it is also possible to feel ex-human.

The men's retreat wasn't just about the emotion of grief. It included back-and-forth Sufi-style poetry readings, with renditions of Yeats, Jeffers, Blake, Li Bai, Ryokan, and Rumi—especially Rumi, the Sufi mystic-poet whose verse has become the bible of the new ritualists and spiritual teachers.

Over the course of the retreat, Michael Meade told us Celtic tales of archetypal fools and heroes, full of symbolic imagery centered on the great themes of life and death. Meade says that these images allow people to connect their personal story to the mythic story. Then, he explains, "There is this immediate relief from the personal. The load is partially carried by the story. Second, a community occurs. What people used to call *communitas.* Everyone winds up connected to the same story, even though they may be connected in different ways."

By the time the retreat was over, I did feel part of a community, however temporary. The same thing happens at meditation retreats and at other workshops I've attended as well. Like meditation practice, ritual and myth can help us step out of our individual drama and also lead us into the common human story, reminding us that we are all united in this moment of evolution, standing on the same plateau of history, sharing the ten thousand joys and sorrows common to our species.

My meditation practice has brought more ease into my life, along with a metaphysics that makes sense to me. But myth, poetry, and ritual are what give vitality to any metaphysics. The men's retreat made me realize that not only do I want a spiritual practice, I want a mythology and rituals that speak to my life here on earth. Even if that mythology is second-hand, even if the rituals are a polyglot, they help to keep me in relationship to the world and teach me how to love it better.

ONE MORE TIME

FRIENDS, BOOMERS, CO-CONSPIRATORS, the alarm bells are sounding again! The barbarians have barged through the gates, the monarch butterflies are departing, and we don't need a weatherman to know the climate's heating up. We're in the midst of environmental collapse, global pandemic, economic inequality and over-the-top greed along with increasing poverty, racism, speech-policing, controlling the bodies of others, and a political polarization that has broken our sense of civility or doing much of anything for the common good.

My dear fellow Boomers, it's time for us to join all good people and come to the aid of our species, our planet, and our galaxy—again!! Let's lead and follow each other, and along with Gen X'ers, Gen Y'ers, Zoomers, and Alphas, and give 'em what we've still got. This call is for you, my friends—and I know you're ready to take to the streets, the airwaves, and social media, to act up and to act out! Many cycles of the sun have passed since we did what was needed then, *and we can do it again.* Let's inspire, join with, and learn from the youngsters, most of whom are over thirty. ("Don't trust anyone over thirty?" OMG, that's us. And *them*!) Even with our bad backs and bum knees, hip replacements and whatever other hitches we have in our giddy-up, let's swallow some Ibuprofen or smear on some CBD, put on our walking shoes, find our old tie-dyed sweatshirts, and get ready to rumble.

Here's one thing you can do: Pick your favorite endangered species and save it. You can read the endangered species list aloud in churches and schools. Otherwise, how will people know? Buy shares in fossil fuel companies and vote to make them grow their solar, wind, and geothermal profit centers. Divest, boycott, stir the pot, and buy local. Go to town meetings and bring affordable housing into your own backyards. Speak up, speak out, join the Squad. Let's get this show on the road.

I, too, was a *retired* radical. I'd turned in my peace symbol and thought I'd ride out my remaining years chilling—listening to public radio, signing petitions, and donating to Clowns without Borders. But the drumbeat is rising *again* in the distance. In 1964 American activist Mario Savio said: "There is a time when the operation of the machine becomes so odious, makes you so sick at heart, that you can't take part! You can't even passively take part! And you've got to put your bodies upon the gears and upon the wheels ... upon the levers, upon all the apparatus, and you've got to make it stop!" And it's true, my fellow Boomers.

Today, almost sixty years later, speech still isn't free, and the patriarchy, though dying slowly, is putting a lock on uteruses and policing our thoughts 24/7. Woody's guitar fought fascists and Arlo told the folks at Alice's Restaurant, "If you want to end war and stuff, you got to sing loud." We do. We got to sing loud.

So dig out those old jeans with actual rips in the knees from when you got knocked down in Chicago and the T-shirt that got torn in the White Night Twinkie riots in San Francisco, and the frog hat you wore at Diablo Canyon protesting nukes. And maybe in the garage you'll find some signs and posters you can use again, like "Make Love, Not War" or "U.S. Out of North America." Or the placard calling for a boycott of grapes. Just paint over "grapes" and call for a boycott of, well, *everything*, or at least unsustainable consumption.

Now get out your guitar or banjo or ukulele and start singing "We Shall Overcome" again! We've had a Clean Air Act, Civil Rights, Voting Rights, Women's Rights, LGBTQ+ Rights, a nuclear freeze, an assault weapons ban, clean elections' bills, and they're all coming undone by greed and the oligarchs' slogan: "Invest in Democracy, Buy a Congressperson."

Fifty-five years ago, we chanted *Om* and watched the Pentagon levitate. Forty years ago, Thich Nhat Hanh and a million of us marched in New York for a nuclear freeze. And now, according to the Council on Foreign Relations' Global Conflict Tracker, there are almost thirty active wars on Mother Earth and two *billion* people live in conflict-affected areas, more than a quarter of the world's population!

We have school shootings and drive-by shootings week after week, planetary die-off is off the rails, the ice caps are melting, and mobs fueled by lies and bigotry stormed the US Capitol. We Boomers still alive and walking and talking and thinking, what can we do to memorialize the values we held so dearly when we were under thirty, when we knew all this was coming?

Friends, Bohemians, Retired Radicals, let's form a Boomer Brigade and protest *everywhere* with our bodies, our investments, our signatures, our voices, and our votes. Take your nap, yes, and then get ready! Get your cane or your walker, and join me. Let's head to the streets chanting, "Hey, Hey, Ho, Ho, all this s--t has got to go." And this time let's really do it with love. The Dalai Lama calls the other side "My friends, the enemy." We're *all* the same species, needing to rethink our thinking and re-act our acting. Our neocortex brought us here, and it's time to tune back into nature and bring back sustainable ways of living on Earth Island. What would Buddha do?

Let's give it what we got one more time and stand up for truth and justice to save our precious planet and ease the suffering of beings everywhere. And, at the same time, let's celebrate the natural miracles within and around us—the mystery of consciousness, the movement of planets and galaxies, and the improbable wonder of it all.

Working alongside our Gen X and Gen Y children, Millennial grandchildren, Zennial great-grandchildren, and precious Alphas, heirs to this mess in all its chaos and beauty, let's do whatever we can however we can wherever we can. *We're all in it together*, and Gaia beckons.

Friends, Comrades, Co-Conspirators, this is Wes "Scoop" Nisker reporting to you from Planet Earth saying, once again: Stay high, but keep your priorities straight. And if you don't like the news, go out and make some of your own!